NEW ORLEANS *Classic* CELEBRATIONS

NEW ORLEANS *Classic* CELEBRATIONS

KIT WOHL

PELICAN PUBLISHING COMPANY

Gretna 2013

The word "Pelican" and the depiction of a pelican
are trademarks of Pelican Publishing Company, Inc.,
and are registered in the
U.S. Patent and Trademark Office.

ISBN: 9781455618330

E-book ISBN: 9781455618347

Printed in China
Published by Pelican Publishing Company, Inc.
1000 Burmaster Street, Gretna, Louisiana 70053

For my brothers, the beekeepers
Robert Brian More & Robert Colin More

CONTENTS

FOREWORD

For most folks, celebrations are those rare and precious occasions when friends and family gather to honor, commemorate or worship special events and traditions or perhaps even persons of other worldly and celestial bearing.

What a shame it is to be those folks. In New Orleans, a celebration is not a page in the family scrapbook or a date circled on a calendar or a distant occasion to be eagerly anticipated.

Celebration is the way of life here—the ubiquitous, near-daily expression of community pride, fellowship and culture. That's why folks come to New Orleans from all over the world to let it all hang out. We talk too much, laugh too loud and live too large. And, frankly, we're suspicious of others who don't.

And we eat.

For all celebrations, all occasions, any event where more than one are gathered. And sometimes even alone. After all, there's no law that says the lonely need suffer the deprivation of repast.

We plan. We prep. We cook. We serve. We eat.

And when we eat, we talk about what we ate last time we were together and, when it's over, we talk about what we'll eat next time. Obsession? No! We just went over this. It's celebration.

Whatever the occasion—particularly our own homegrown and adapted events and holidays—we've likely got our own music for it, because we do everything to music. And we've probably established a dress code for it, because we costume or suitably attire for everything.

We've definitely got our own cuisine for it, because meals are our central bonding ritual, food is our cultural currency. It is what we offer to our hosts and deliver to our guests, what we share to affirm our union.

The recipes in this book are an entrée into the central social activity of all New Orleans celebrations. With these, you are treated to the sights, smells and tastes that enliven any gathering of locals—from the patrician cotillions of Uptown to the Sunday afternoon second line parades back-a-town.

Some folks are always asking: Why does everything in New Orleans have to be about food?

Of course, we respond: Why isn't everything everywhere about food? After all, you could live without music and clothing if you absolutely had to.

But we don't advise that. At least, not the music part. It's the old eat-to-live/live-to-eat conundrum. We solve it with another slightly abridged adage from the American almanac: When life gives you lemons...make icebox pie. Or citrus salad. Or even daiquiris. But lemonade? Seriously? It goes without saying: There is no place quite like New Orleans. That's why we say it so much.

Yes, by now some folks around the country have grown tired of hearing New Orleanians go on and on about how theirs is the most interesting city in America.

Well: This just in. It is. So get over it. Get into it. Best to start with a knife and fork.

And some fitting recipes.

— **Chris Rose**

REVEILLON *and* HOLIDAYS

Although we can never promise the frosty noses and red cheeks of Norman Rockwell's American Christmas ideal, New Orleans by no means lacks the amenities of the season.

The historic streetcars are festooned with garlands of evergreen and red ribbons. The massive Superdome, set in the heart of downtown, serves as the screen for the dazzling, pulsing red-and-green nightly light show.

Massive wooden bonfire structures are constructed atop the Mississippi River levees, a centuries-old ritual intended to light the way downriver for Papa Noel and his cargo of gifts.

It's the season of Reveillon, the French word for "awakening," the robust meal that was once prepared to revive the senses after Midnight Mass on Christmas Eve. It's now a popular seasonal tradition at local restaurants at more conventional dining hours to accommodate both citizenry and visitors.

The fare is warm, hearty, and built for comfort—four- and five-course meals bearing the treasures of our waters, our farms, and our forests. The signature dish of the season is the turducken, the pride of any self-respecting south Louisiana butcher: a de-boned chicken stuffed inside a de-boned duck stuffed inside a de-boned turkey.

The turducken may sound like something from a Marx Brothers comedy routine, but is actually the centerpiece of grand dining celebrations from the cottages of Cajun country to the mansions along the St. Charles streetcar line.

New Orleans went into a flap when Chef Paul Prudhomme reintroduced the turducken. Its local origins are murky, with numerous cooks highlighting their own creations. Following NFL sportscaster John Madden's aside during a Monday Night Football broadcast, the phoenix of poultry began landing on tables everywhere. Noted in American Cooking: Creole and Acadian (1971), a chef at Corrine Dunbar's used nine different birds.

The turducken concept has evolved from Roman times, through the Middle Ages and Victorian era. In Trimalchio's account of a Roman feast, a boar was slit open and out flew live birds. The 19th-century French did it more often in galantines, as chronicled in the famous L'Oreiller de la Belle Aurore recipe described in Lucien Tendret's 1892 "La Table au Pays de Brillat-Savarin" cookbook. Before the Turducken, the Rôti Sans Pareil was made by chef Grimod de La Reniere in 1807, and that consisted of seventeen different birds being cooked inside each other. A galantine is a big 'pillow' of various birds and animals.

CHARLIE HOHORST III, CAJUN GROCER
TURDUCKEN

In a city of fantastical appetites, it makes perfect sense that we would bag and serve that most rare of hybrid birds, the turducken. The turducken, as the name suggests, is in fact a deboned chicken inside a deboned duck inside a deboned turkey. And in between each layer of meat there is a layer of delicious stuffing.

Begin at least two days in advance, boning the poultry and making the dressings. Then keep each component separate, tightly covered and refrigerated.

Take shortcuts, such as asking a butcher to bone the birds for you and three good friends to each produce a different stuffing.

The three stuffings may be any compatible favorites, so long as each has a distinctive taste and texture. Finish with gravy made from the pan juices.

SERVES 10 to 12

a 20-25 pound turkey, deboned, with wings and legs still intact
2-3 tablespoons poultry seasoning (see page 90)
cornbread stuffing (see page 15)
a 5-6 pound duckling, deboned
Cajun rice stuffing (see page 15)
a 3-4 pound chicken, deboned
shrimp stuffing (see page 15)

1. Flatten the turkey, skin side down, and rub the top with poultry seasoning. Spread the cornbread stuffing over the turkey in a layer about 1/2-inch thick. (If you exactly follow the recipes for the stuffings listed above, you will have leftovers from all of them. Place the leftovers in 3 separate casserole dishes, bake at 350 degrees for about 30 minutes, and serve with the turducken.)

2. Place the duckling, skin side down, on the cornbread stuffing and spread a 1/2-inch-thick layer of Cajun rice stuffing over the top.

3. Place the chicken, skin side down, on the Cajun rice stuffing and spread a 1/2-inch-thick layer of shrimp stuffing over the top.

4. With kitchen twine and a needle, stitch the birds closed (the stitches about 1 inch apart), starting at the neck. It is helpful for someone else to hold the birds together while you stitch. Finish by tying the legs together just above the tip bone.

5. Preheat oven to 325 degrees. Place the assembled turducken, breast side up, in a roasting pan and cook until a thermometer inserted into the thickest part registers 180 degrees. This should take around 4 1/2 to 5 hours.

6. Let the turducken cool and slice it across from side to side, like a cake, so that everyone gets some of each bird.

Ready to cook turducken and other Louisiana specialties are available at www.cajungrocer.com.

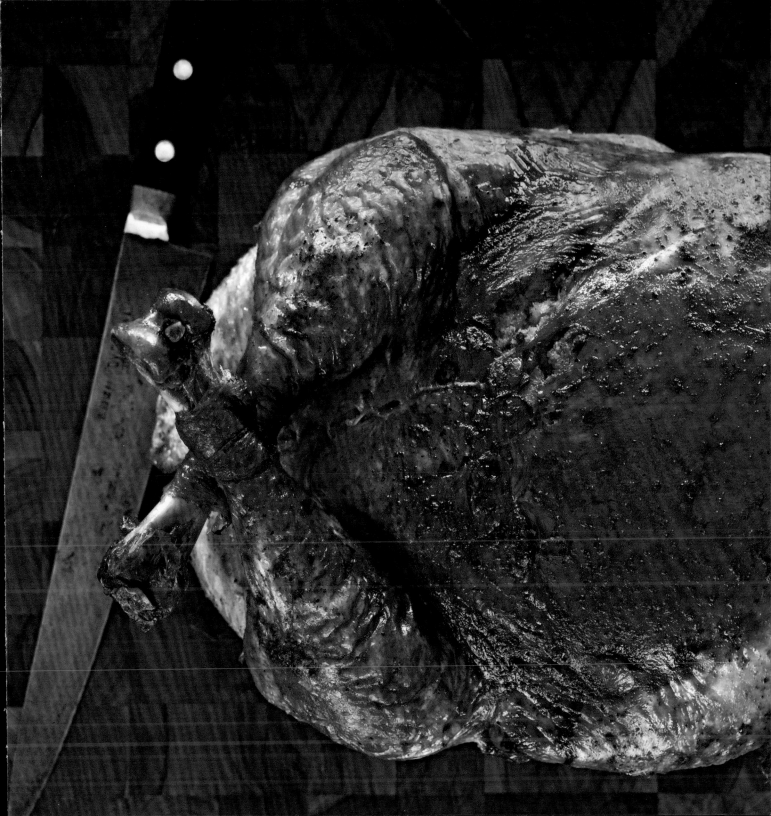

SHRIMP STUFFING
MAKES about 8 cups

2 tablespoons cooking oil
1 cup chopped onion
1/2 cup chopped green bell pepper
1 cup chopped celery
1 clove garlic, minced
10 ounces canned diced tomatoes
2 pounds raw shrimp, chopped
4 cups cooked white rice
salt and freshly ground black pepper to taste
dash of cayanne pepper to taste

1. In a large saucepan heat oil and sauté the onion, bell pepper, celery, and garlic until soft. Add the tomatoes and heat through.

2. Add the shrimp and cook until the shrimp turn slightly pink.

3. Stir in the cooked rice, season to taste with salt, pepper, and cayenne.

CAJUN RICE STUFFING

MAKES about 8 cups

2 tablespoons cooking oil
1 pound ground beef
1 cup chopped bell pepper
1 cup chopped onion
1 cup chopped celery
1 clove garlic, minced
salt and pepper to taste
11 ounces cream of mushroom soup
4 cups cooked white rice
2 cups beef broth

1. In a large saucepan heat cooking oil and brown the ground beef over medium heat.

2. Add bell pepper, onion, celery, and garlic and cook until all the vegetables have softened. Season to taste.

3. Add the mushroom soup and heat through.

4. Stir in the cooked rice and pour in the beef broth until it reaches the desired consistency.

CORNBREAD STUFFING
MAKES about 8 cups

2 tablespoons cooking oil
1/2 pound chicken livers, chopped
1/2 pound chicken gizzards, chopped
1 cup chopped celery
1 cup chopped onion
1 cup chopped bell pepper
4 cups cornbread, crumbled
2 cups chicken broth
poultry seasoning to taste
salt and freshly ground black pepper to taste

1. In a large saucepan heat the cooking oil and brown the chopped livers and gizzards over medium heat. Add the celery, onion, and bell pepper and cook until soft.

2. Add the crumbled cornbread to the meat and vegetables. Stir in chicken broth until the mixture reaches the desired consistency and adjust seasoning.

CHEF GUS MARTIN, MURIEL'S
MURIEL'S OYSTER STUFFING

MAKES 1 1/2 quarts

1/2 pound (2 sticks) unsalted butter
1 tablespoon minced garlic
1/2 cup diced green bell pepper
1 cup diced yellow onion
1/2 cup diced celery
1 1/2 teaspoons dried thyme
2 bay leaves
24 freshly shucked oysters, coursely chopped

4 1/2 cups course bread crumbs
1 tablespoon salt
1/2 teaspoon freshly ground black pepper
1 bunch green onions, finely chopped

1. Preheat oven to 350 degrees. In a medium saucepan over medium-high heat, melt the butter. Add the garlic, bell pepper, onion, celery, thyme, and bay leaves and cook until the vegetables have softened.

2. Reduce the heat to medium, add the oysters, and cook for 5 minutes. Fold in the bread crumbs, salt, black pepper, and green onions and cook, stirring occasionally, until the greens onions are softened.

3. Transfer the stuffing to a 2-quart casserole dish and bake for 20 minutes, or until the bread crumbs are lightly browned and the dressing is heated through. Serve warm.

CHEF CHIP FLANAGAN, RALPH'S ON THE PARK
LOUISIANA CITRUS SALAD

Many farms around the city produce luscious citrus, generally appearing at the outdoor markets during the holiday season. Colorful and tangy, Chef Flanagan's salad is a colorfully refreshing accompaniment to heartier fare.

SERVES 4 to 6

1 satsuma
1 ruby red grapefruit
1 Meyer lemon
1 lime
1 small shallot, julienned
1 tablespoon honey
1/4 bunch of cilantro, washed well and chopped
1/2 tablespoon kosher salt

1. Remove the skin and white pith from the satsuma, grapefruit, lemon, and lime and separate the fruit into segments.

2. Working over a large mixing bowl, make a small "V" cut into the side of each segment and place in the bowl.

3. Mix the fruit in the bowl with all the other ingredients and serve immediately.

At City Park, across the street from Ralph's on the Park, Celebration in the Oaks is a festive stroll through gardens of sparkling moss-draped trees, lighted figurines, a model train display, and nightly performances.

Ralph Brennan is another of this generation's Brennan cousins who has made a significant impact on the hospitality scene. In addition to the old casino building next door to City Park, he created the popular Redfish Grill in the French Quarter, Heritage Grill, Café b, Café NOMA, and Jazz Kitchen.

GINNY WARREN, MISS GINNY'S ROOST
WILD SWEET POTATO CASSEROLE
with PECAN STREUSEL TOPPING

There is not much more traditional than sweet potatoes for the holidays. This recipe adds a nice tangy note to the standard with the addition of Wild Turkey bourbon-soaked apricots.

SERVES 8 to 10

3 large sweet potatoes
1 pound dried apricots
1 cup Wild Turkey bourbon
3 sticks unsalted butter, at room temperature, cut into cubes
1 cup pecan pieces
1 cup dark brown sugar
1/4 cup flour

1. Preheat oven to 350 degrees. Bake the sweet potatoes in their skins until soft, about 1 hour. Keep oven heated.

2. While sweet potatoes are baking, place the apricots and bourbon in a 1-quart saucepan. Add enough water to cover the apricots and simmer on low heat until the apricots are soft, about 30 minutes. Remove from heat and let stand until cool and the sweet potatoes are done.

3. Let potatoes cool and remove the skins. Transfer the potatoes, apricots, and any left-over liquid to a food processor. Add 2/3 of the butter cubes and blend the mixture until smooth.

4. Transfer the mixture to an oven-safe 9- by 13-inch glass baking dish and smooth the top to roughly level with a rubber spatula.

5. In a small mixing bowl, mix the pecan pieces, brown sugar, flour, and remaining 1/3 butter until crumbly and sprinkle over the top of the sweet-potato mixture.

6. Bake the casserole for 30 minutes, or until lightly browned.

NOTE: Bourbon, rum, cognac, or the spirits of your choice can be substituted, or eliminated.

Ginny Warren transplanted her New Orleans sensibilities and culinary expertise to Miss Ginny's Roost in Pavillion, Wyoming, no kidding. There, she runs her small restaurant, rides horseback, and brands calves. Here, she left her mark at the Royal Sonesta, Restaurant Jonathan, Arnaud's, and other outstanding establishments. The only riding she did in New Orleans was Molly's St. Patrick's Day parade.

She missed New Orleans' recent snow. She called it a flurry. We called it a snow storm.

She continues to spread New Orleans' culinary word of mouth by adding her Creole and Cajun specialties to the Roost's menu.

Known as the Grande Dame of French Quarter restaurants, Arnaud's celebrated a legend's return to grandeur when Archie and Jane Casbarian restored the establishment in 1979, giving the family owned and operated Creole establishment new life. Encompassing 13 historic French Quarter buildings, a restaurant as venerable as Arnaud's sometimes has quirky ways of doing things, holding dear small rituals and courtesies that distinguish it, such as using crumbers to scrape away bits of crusty bread left tabletop.

Executive chef Tommy DiGiovanni, a native New Orleanian, has spent most of his life in a kitchen.

(recipe continued from right)

8. Mix the remaining egg yolk with the cream and brush the mixture over the top of the puff pastry dough.

9. Bake for 15-20 minutes, or until the pastry turns golden brown.

CHEF TOMMY DiGIOVANNI, ARNAUD'S
CREOLE ONION SOUP

Served as a Reveillon menu item, this elegant creamy onion soup releases a fragrant cloud when the pastry top is pierced.

SERVES 4

1/2 stick unsalted butter
2 yellow onions, thinly sliced
1 cup white wine
1 cup chicken stock
1 bay leaf
1 sprig fresh thyme
6 black peppercorns
1/4 gallon veal stock
1/2 – 3/4 cup blond roux (see page 88)
salt and freshly ground black pepper to taste
13 ounces puff pastry dough
2 egg yolks
1 tablespoon water
1-2 tablespoons cream

1. In a stockpot, melt the butter over medium-high heat. Add the onion slices and cook, stirring constantly, until they are a golden color, about 15 minutes.

2. Add the wine, chicken stock, bay leaf, thyme, and peppercorns. Deglaze until most of the liquid has evaporated.

3. Add the veal stock to the pot and let simmer for about 10 minutes.

4. Add 1/2 cup of roux and simmer the soup, stirring constantly, until the roux is evenly mixed in. (If you want a thicker soup, add the remaining roux.) Simmer for 20 minutes, season with salt and pepper to taste, and set aside to cool.

5. On a lightly floured surface, roll the puff pastry dough out to 1/8 inch thick. Using an individual bowl or ramekin that the soup will be served in, cut out 4 circles of pastry slightly larger than the opening of the bowls. Fill the bowls or ramekins about 3/4 full of soup.

6. Mix 1 egg yolk with the water and rub around the edge of the bowls or ramekins. Then cover with the puff pastry dough, pulling the dough lightly over the opening. Be careful not to let the dough fall into the soup. Refrigerate for one hour.

7. Preheat oven to 400 degrees. Remove the ramekins from the refrigerator and let them come to room temperature.

(recipe continued at left)

CHEF JOHN BESH, RESTAURANT AUGUST
GNOCCHI, CRAB *and* TRUFFLE

Gnocchi with fresh crab and black truffle creates a dish of subtle balanced flavors.

SERVES 6 to 8

FOR THE GNOCCHI
2 1/2 pounds Yukon gold potatoes, peeled and quartered
4 teaspoons butter
5 large grade A egg yolks
1 3/4 all-purpose flour
1 dash fresh grated nutmeg
salt to taste
white pepper to taste
olive oil for coating the gnocci

FOR THE SAUCE
1 tablespoon olive oil
4 teaspoons minced shallot
1/2 cup vermouth
3 tablespoons unsalted fish stock
1/2 cup heavy cream
1 tablespoon unsalted butter
1 cup lump crabmeat
1/4 teaspoon white truffle oil
salt to taste
shaved fresh black truffle, for garnish
shaved Parmigiano-Reggiano cheese, for garnish

Make the Gnocchi

1. Preheat oven to 250 degrees. Place the potatoes in an oven-safe pot and cover with water. Cook over high heat until tender, about 15 to 20 minutes. Drain the water from the pot and cook in the oven for another 15 minutes.

2. Pass the potatoes through a potato ricer into a fine mesh sieve. Using a rubber spatula, press the potatoes through the sieve into a clean mixing bowl. Add the butter and egg yolks, mixing well. Fold in the flour gradually until a manageable dough is formed. Fold in the nutmeg, and season to taste with salt and white pepper.

3. Separate a fist-size ball of dough from rest and gently roll out on a lightly floured surface until uniformly 3/4 inch thick. Cut into 3/4-inch lengths and roll each length into a ball. Working quickly, shape with a gnocchi board and drop into simmering salted water. Once the gnocchi float, simmer 15 to 20 seconds and transfer to ice bath. Once cold, remove and toss in olive oil to coat. Use that day or freeze.

(recipe continued at right)

Besh's talent and drive have earned him continual kudos including the James Beard Award for Best Chef - Southeast in 2006. His nine restaurants (August, Besh Steak, Lüke, Lüke San Antonio, La Provence, American Sector, Soda Shop, Domenica, and Borgne) each celebrate the traditions of the region in their own unique way. August was nominated in 2012 and 2013 for the James Beard Outstanding Restaurant award.

(recipe continued from left)
Make the Sauce

1. In a large saucepan, heat the olive oil over medium heat. Add the shallots and cook until they begin to sweat. Remove the pan from heat and add the vermouth. Return to heat and bring to a boil. Add fish stock and bring back to a boil. Add cream, reduce heat, and bring to a simmer. Pass the sauce through a fine mesh sieve to remove the shallot and return to a clean pot.

2. Add the gnocchi and butter to the pot and cook until the gnocchi are heated through and the sauce has thickened. Stir in the crab and truffle oil, heating just until the crab is warmed through. Season to taste with salt. Serve in warm bowls, garnished with shaved black truffle and Parmigiano-Reggiano.

Chef Donald Link drives the concept behind Herbsaint, a small bistro serving big flavors born of his Louisiana heritage. He is opinionated about some things, especially the high flavor profiles he creates from his state's bounty. He presides over his tiny Warehouse District restaurant, Herbsaint.

He is a James Beard Foundation honoree as Best Chef, Southeast, 2007 and was nominated in 2013 for the James Beard Outstanding Chef award, in addition to a slew of other local and national honors. Both restaurants have received recognition for culinary excellence. Forbes magazine named Chef Link a Top Ten Chef to Watch, and New Orleans magazine called him Chef of the Year. He can be found in the Herbsaint kitchen, unless he is over at Cochon, Butcher, or Peche, his other restaurants.

(recipe continued from right)
Make the Grit Cakes

1. Add the jalapeño and Parmigiano-Reggiano to the pot of prepared grits and mix thoroughly. Grease a 10- by 15-inch baking pan that is at least 1 inch deep, pour the grits into the pan, and chill, covered, for at least 1 hour to set.

2. Preheat the oven to 350 degrees. Bake the grits for about 20 minutes, or until they are hot and crisp on the bottom. Using a wet knife, cut the grits into 3-inch squares.

3. To serve, place a square of grits on each plate. Spoon about a tablespoon of gravy over them and top with the shrimp. Garnish with parsley or chives.

SHRIMP, GREEN CHILI GRITS *and* TASSO CREAM

SERVES 8 small plates or 4 entrées

FOR THE SHRIMP *and* GRAVY

4 tablespoons butter	1 cup shrimp stock
1/2 cup diced onion	1 cup heavy cream
1/2 cup diced celery	a dash of lemon juice
1/2 cup diced tasso ham	a dash of hot sauce
1 tablespoon chopped thyme	3 tablespoons olive oil
3/4 teaspoon cayenne pepper	2 pounds large fresh shrimp, peeled and deveined
3/4 teaspoon paprika	1 1/2 teaspoons salt
1 teaspoon chopped garlic	1 1/2 teaspoons freshly ground black pepper
4 tablespoons flour	parsley or chives for garnish

FOR THE GRIT CAKES

1 jalapeño pepper, seeded and finely chopped
1/2 cup finely grated Parmigiano-Reggiano cheese
3 cups cooked grits, prepared according the package directions*

*5-minute grits and regular grits are recommended over instant for quality.

Make the Shrimp and Gravy

1. Melt 2 tablespoons of the butter in a medium saucepan over medium heat. Add the onion, celery, ham, thyme, cayenne, paprika, and garlic and cook the vegetables, stirring occasionally, until they are soft. Add the remaining butter and when it has melted, add the flour, stirring well to mix the flour in with the vegetables.

2. Add the shrimp stock gradually and cook until the sauce has reduced by half. (Whenever making sauce that has some sort of roux, add liquids in stages so that the sauce doesn't become too thin. It's always easier to thin a sauce if needed than to thicken it.) Add the cream and reduce, stirring occasionally, until the texture is thick. Remove the gravy from the heat and stir in the lemon juice and hot sauce.

3. In a large saucepan, heat the olive oil over medium heat until it is hot but not smoking. Add the shrimp, cook for about 2 minutes on each side, or until almost cooked through, and drain any excess oil from the pan. Pour the reserved gravy over the shrimp, reduce the heat to low, and simmer for another 5 minutes. Stir in salt and pepper.

(recipe continued at left)

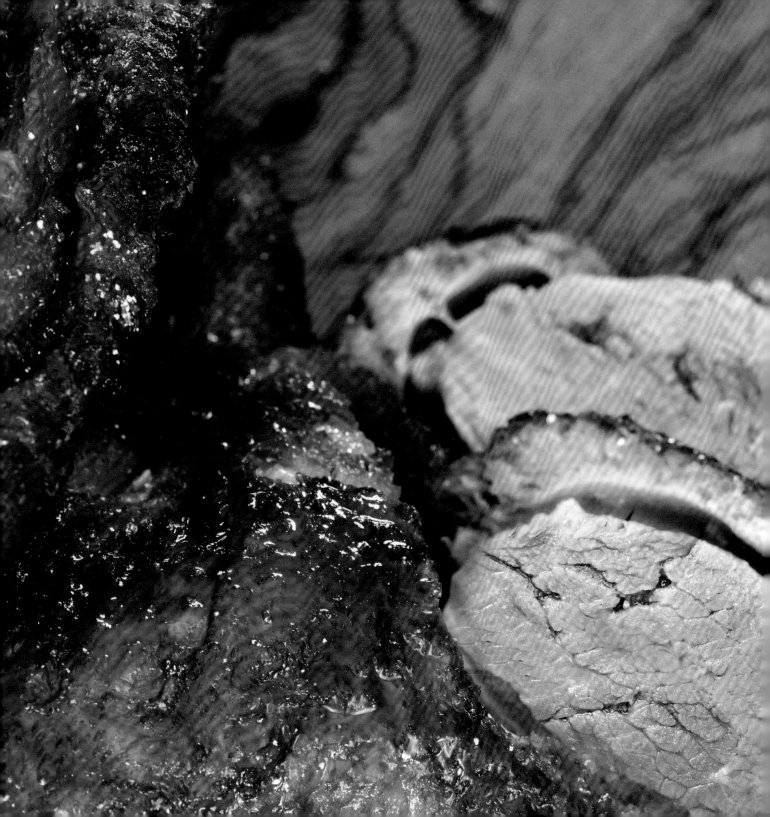

CHEF SUSAN SPICER, BAYONA
ROASTED DUCK
with ORANGE CANE-SYRUP SAUCE

Bayona's style is pure serendipity with a dash of Big Easy flavor.

SERVES 2 to 4

FOR THE DUCKLING
a 5-pound duckling
1 onion, quartered
1 medium orange (or Satsuma, a Louisiana mandarin), zested (reserving the zest),
quartered, and pips discarded
1 teaspoon chopped fresh sage
1 teaspoon chopped fresh thyme
1 teaspoon salt
1/2 teaspoon freshly ground black pepper

FOR THE ORANGE CANE-SYRUP SAUCE
2 cups fresh-squeezed orange or satsuma juice
1 cup cane vinegar or apple cider vinegar
2 medium shallots, minced
1/4 cup cane syrup
2 cups chicken stock
2 tablespoons butter, softened

Prepare the Duckling

1. Rinse the duckling under running water, pat it dry, and trim away some of the excess fat around the cavity. Stuff the bird with the onion and orange quarters and tie the legs closed with string.

2. In a small bowl, mix together the orange zest, sage, thyme, salt, and black pepper. Prick the skin lightly all over and rub generously with the herb mixture. Set the duckling aside at room temperature for 1 hour or refrigerate overnight.

3. Place a 13- by 9-inch roasting pan in the oven. Preheat oven to 425 degrees.

4. Place the duckling, breast side up, in the preheated roasting pan and roast for 30 minutes. Reduce the heat to 400 degrees. Turn the duckling over, baste, and roast for 30 minutes more. Turn the duckling so it is breast-side up again, baste, and roast for 30 minutes more, or until skin is crisp and juices run clear when you prick the thigh. Remove from the heat and let rest for 10 minutes.

Begin the sauce as soon as the duck is in the oven.

(recipe continued at right)

Susan was named by the James Beard Foundation in 1993 as Best Chef, Southeast, and in 2010 she was inducted into the James Beard Foundation's Who's Who of Food and Beverage in America.

Bayona is another good reason New Orleans attracts food lovers from around the world. Susan Spicer earned her culinary chops as an apprentice in New Orleans. Forming a partnership with Regina Keever, Bayona opened in a beautiful, 200-year-old cottage in the French Quarter.

(recipe continued from left)
Make the Orange Cane-Syrup Sauce

1. In a small saucepan bring to a boil the orange juice, vinegar, and shallots. Reduce the heat to a simmer until the liquid is reduced to about 1 cup and whisk in the cane syrup. Pour half of the mixture into a small bowl, reserving it for basting the duckling.

2. In another saucepan, bring the chicken stock to a boil, reduce the heat to a simmer, and cook until the stock is reduced to about 1/2 a cup. Whisk in remaining half of the juice mixture and simmer for about 7 minutes, or until slightly syrupy.

3. Whisk in the butter, a tablespoon at a time, until you have a light, creamy sauce. Taste for seasoning and add a little more salt if necessary. The sauce should be balanced between sweet and tart. If too tart, add a little more syrup. Set aside while the duckling finishes roasting.

Serve the duckling whole or remove the breasts and legs, serving the breast meat sliced and the legs whole. Spoon the orange sauce over the duckling or serve warm on the side.

Riverboat gamblers rolled on the Mississippi in 1840, when young Antoine Alciatore started Antoine's, now America's oldest family-operated restaurant. Rick Blount, the fifth-generation chief executive officer, maintains his ancestor's traditions as tradition-minded New Orleans maintain their habits—of which Antoine's is one.

The rambling facility is testament to French Creole New Orleans, a snapshot of period architecture and decor festooned with a kaleidoscope of historic memorabilia, photographs, and clippings. A number of benchmark dishes were created there, including Oysters Rockefeller, for which the recipe has never been divulged. They insist it does not contain spinach but a variety of other green vegetables.

Antoine's celebrates Mardi Gras, with their Rex Room and carnival luncheons. Until recently menus were printed only in French, but everyone knew the specialties. Antoine's is treasured for local habits, a private New Orleanians' entrance, and personal family waiters—a position often passed down from generation to generation of both.

Most certainly, almost every guest is familiar with the jolly harlequin, or jester, as you choose to believe, who holds the brûlot bowl aloft. It is a traditional finale for a grand meal.

CHEF MICHAEL REGUA, SR., ANTOINE'S
BAKED ALASKA

Few celebrations are complete without Antoine's Baked Alaska.

SERVES 8 to 12
a 9-inch-across circular sponge cake
1 quart ice cream, traditionally vanilla
6 egg whites, at room temperature
1/2 teaspoon fresh lemon juice
6 tablespoons granulated sugar
2 tablespoons brandy
1 cup chocolate sauce for serving

1. If making the sponge cake yourself, prepare it the night before and refrigerate overnight. Also the night before, leave the ice cream out until it has softened and can be easily scooped. Press the ice cream into a 1-quart metal mixing bowl about 8 inches across, smoothing the top to flatten, and chill, covered, in the freezer.

2. About an hour before the dish is to be served, remove the bowl of ice cream from the freezer and place it in a bath of hot water that reaches almost to the top of the bowl. Place the sponge cake on a heatproof platter and as soon as the ice cream can slide in the bowl, turn it out onto the sponge cake, dome side up. Put the platter with the cake and ice cream back in the freezer.

3. Place the oven rack on its lowest setting and preheat the broiler. In a medium mixing bowl, beat the egg whites with the lemon juice until they have almost begun forming soft peaks and gradually add the sugar in a steady stream, beating constantly until stiff peaks form.

4. Remove the cake and ice cream from the freezer. Working quickly, use a rubber spatula to coat the ice-cream dome and cake with most of the meringue, swirling to create a wavy surface. Reserve some of the meringue in a pastry bag to be piped on after baking.

5. Place the platter under the broiler, watching it constantly and turning it a couple of times if necessary for even browning, for 2 to 3 minutes, or until the meringue is a golden brown.

6. Pipe an edge of the reserved meringue around the base of the dome. If you're feeling ambitious, you can pipe on a name or date as well.

7. Just before serving, warm the brandy and proceed directly to the table. Pour the warmed brandy into a large pre-warmed ladle, set light to it with a long match, and drizzle the flaming brandy around the edge of the Baked Alaska. Scoop individual portions into bowls and serve with the chocolate sauce, warmed, in a gravy boat as an accompaniment.

PHUNNY PHORTY PHELLOWS, MARDI GRAS *and* CARNIVAL

It's only natural that a port city settled by outcasts, thieves, rogues, and pirates would not shy away from stealing cultural treasures as well as monetary. Especially when the booty amounts to another reason to dance, mask, and feast. (Cultural piracy, shall we say?)

New Orleans didn't invent Mardi Gras. But we did set out to stamp the celebration indelibly, make it our own signature event, and it's now the biggest and the best Carnival display in North America.

Unfortunately, it seems like lots of folks in the Heartland think Mardi Gras is a lewd and bestial bacchanal among consenting adults—a lawless, boozy street party with no limits or decency. And, OK, it can be that. In some quarters.

But the truth is that Mardi Gras is the love of life as uniquely expressed in South Louisiana. It is the harmonic convergence of our food, music, creativity, tolerance, eccentricity, our neighborhoods, and our joy of living—all at once.

Friends and families stake out the same viewing spots along parade routes year after year. Those lucky enough to live along the traditional routes often open their homes to friends and family in a week-long pot-luck jamboree. Plates of jambalaya, tureens of gumbo and King Cakes appear and disappear with each new crowd. Princess Shiloh Sanders (left) contemplates a royal spread.

Mardi Gras is no time for long, languishing meals. Food at Carnival time is not just for human sustenance, but for fuel to carry the revelers through this one-of-kind New Orleans celebration.

A finalist for the James Beard Foundation's Best Chef South, 2013, Justin Devillier works with Mia Freiberger-Devillier, his wife, at their La Petite Grocery.

For nearly 70 years, Von der Haar's Fine Foods was an institution in New Orleans at the Magazine Street address that is now La Petite Grocery's. Von der Haar's Fine Foods also delivered, which made them a hit around here, especially at my house. Those were the good old days.

For the good new days, the converted space has been renovated into a clean-lined, French-style bistro with menus to match. La Petite Grocery's interior is lined with pressed-tin ceilings and dark woods, but food is the focus, as it should be in this location.

ROASTED GARLIC AIOLI

YIELDS 1 cup

2 egg yolks
1 clove garlic, minced
1 teaspoon kosher salt
1/4 teaspoon freshly ground black pepper
1 tablespoon lemon juice
1 cup canola oil
1/4 cup olive oil

Blend all ingredients together except the oil. Slowly pour in both oils and blend well.

CHEF JUSTIN DEVILLIER, LA PETITE GROCERY
LOUISIANA BLUE CRAB BEIGNETS

Savory beignets are a takeoff on the better-known sugar-coated variety. La Petite Grocery makes them with crab meat, but shrimp or crawfish would also be delicious.

SERVES 6

1/4 pound jumbo lump crab meat (preferably Louisiana blue crabs)
1/4 pound Mascarpone cheese
2 tablespoons chopped chives
1/2 French shallot, finely minced
salt and freshly ground black pepper to taste
1 cup all-purpose white flour (preferably Wondra instant flour)
1 cup plus 1 tablespoon cornstarch
1 tablespoon baking powder
1 cup beer
2 quarts peanut oil or good quality vegetable oil, for frying

1. In a medium mixing bowl, thoroughly mix crab meat, Mascarpone, chives, shallot, and salt and pepper. Shape into small balls approximately the diameter of a quarter and refrigerate, covered, for 1 hour.

2. In a large mixing bowl, mix together the flour, cornstarch, baking powder, and beer until mixed well but still lumpy.

3. In an electric deep-fryer or heavy-bottomed skillet, heat the oil to 375 degrees.

4. Dredge the chilled crab meat balls through the flour mixture, taking care to coat them completely. Add them gently, one at a time, to the heated oil so that they don't touch. Be careful not to burn yourself.

5. Fry the crab balls until golden brown, about 2 to 3 minutes. Remove them with a sieve or slotted spoon and drain on paper towels. Serve with Roasted Garlic Aioli for dipping. *(Recipe at left)*

POPPY TOOKER
SHRIMP CALAS *with* GARLIC MAYONNAISE

Calas is a time-honored culinary tradition in the Creole community, particularly in the predominantly African American Treme neighborhood. Calas may also be made as a savory by bits of leftover meat. Poppy's "Eat it to Save it" initiative has helped bring it to the forefront.

SERVES 4 to 6

FOR THE GARLIC MAYONNAISE
3 cloves garlic
1/2 bunch scallions
1 egg
juice of 1 lemon
1 cup olive oil
1/2 cup parsley
2 tablespoons ketchup

FOR THE SHRIMP CALAS
2 cups cooked rice
8 tablespoons flour
3 scallions, thinly sliced
4 tablespoons chopped boiled shrimp
2 teaspoons baking powder
1/4 teaspoon salt
1 tablespoons Louisiana hot sauce
2 eggs, whisked
vegetable oil for frying

To make the Garlic Mayonnaise

1. In a food processor finely chop the garlic cloves and scallions.

2. Turn off the food processor and add the egg and lemon juice. Turn the processor back on and slowly drizzle in the olive oil until the mixture is well blended.

3. Mix in the parsley and ketchup by pulsing quickly. Store in a refrigerator for several hours before serving to allow the flavors to blend.

To make the Shrimp Calas

1. In a mixing bowl, stir together the rice, flour, scallion, shrimp, baking powder, and salt.

2. Carefully fold the hot sauce and eggs into the rice mixture until fully incorporated.

3. In a heavy-bottomed skillet or fryer, bring the oil to 360 degrees. Carefully

(recipe continued at right)

"Have mercy, Poppy!" Wynton Marsalis begged on the Superbowl Sunday edition of CBS Sunday Morning as he sampled Poppy's cooking. She's champion of Louisiana's culinary customs, cookbook author, and host of the NPR-affiliated "Louisiana Eats."

Active in the Southern Foodways Alliance, Poppy is sought after for speaking and cooking demonstrations.

(recipe continued from left)

drop spoonfuls of batter into the hot oil, making sure not to splatter oil. Cook the calas in batches so as not to crowd them. In between batches, allow the oil to return to 360 degrees.

4. Let the calas brown, about 1 or 2 minutes, and flip them with tongs or a spatula to cook the other side.

5. After the second side has browned, remove the calas using a sieve or slotted spoon. Serve immediately with the garlic mayonnaise for dipping.

(recipe continued from right)

Make the Fried Chicken

1. If using an electric fryer, set the temperature to 350 degrees and add the peanut oil. If not, heat the oil to 350 degrees in a deep, heavy-bottomed frying pan or Dutch oven.

2. Using two large rectangular or oval roasting pans, fill one with buttermilk and the other with flour.

3. Dip each piece of chicken into the flour and shake it lightly to remove the excess flour. Then dip it in the buttermilk, being sure to soak it completely. Coat each piece again with flour, but do not shake off the excess.

4. Add the chicken pieces to the oil, in batches (being careful not to burn yourself) so that there is space between the pieces, and cook the chicken until the batter has turned golden brown, about 3 to 5 minutes for the smaller pieces.

5. As the chicken pieces finish cooking, use tongs to transfer them to a plate lined with paper towels to drain.

6. When all the chicken is cooked, add to the gumbo base, one piece at a time. Season with salt and pepper to taste and divide among 6 large shallow bowls over the white rice.

CHEF GARY DARLING, THE TASTE BUDS
FRIED CHICKEN GUMBO

Gumbo is served almost everywhere, every season, but perhaps not anytime more often than during Carnival. Fried chicken is also a Mardi Gras standard, so either or both make perfect sense for parade guests. Chef Gary Darling dreamed up fried chicken gumbo in a head to head Tennessee Williams Festival throw down. Certainly any fried chicken will work for this special gumbo but a shortcut uses Popeyes intense flavors to add some extra zippity do dah.

SERVES 4 to 6

FOR THE GUMBO BASE
1 1/2 cups vegetable oil
2 cups all-purpose flour
2 large onions, chopped
4 celery stalks, chopped
3 green bell peppers, chopped
4 quarts salt-free chicken stock, fresh or canned
1 sprig fresh rosemary
1 teaspoon dried sage, rubbed
1 teaspoon dried thyme
1/4 teaspoon cayenne pepper

FOR THE FRIED CHICKEN
2 quarts peanut oil
2 quarts buttermilk (preferably Bulgarian style)
1 pound self-rising flour
1 whole raw chicken (skin and bones removed), cut into pieces
salt and freshly ground black pepper to taste

enough freshly cooked white rice for 6

Make the Gumbo Base

1. In a large heavy saucepan over low heat, cook the vegetable oil and flour, stirring frequently, to create a roux. Continue cooking, taking care not to let the roux burn, for 30 to 40 minutes, or until the roux has turned a deep mahogany brown.

2. Add the onion, celery, and bell pepper, and cook until the vegetables are translucent and tender. (The roux will continue to darken while this happens.)

3. In a separate saucepan, warm the chicken stock. Gradually add it to the roux, stirring to incorporate well.

4. Add the rosemary, sage, thyme, and cayenne. Stir well and let simmer, covered, while preparing the fried chicken. *(recipe continued at left)*

CHEF LEAH CHASE, DOOKY CHASE'S
STUFFED MIRLITONS

We call them mirlitons, others think of them as chayote squash. Stuffed with savory ingredients and seasoned, it is an inspired main course or a side.

SERVES 6

3 large mirlitons
1/4 cup (1/2 stick) unsalted butter
1/4 pound ground smoked ham
1/2 cup chopped onions
1/2 pound shrimp, peeled, veined, and chopped
2 tablespoons chopped scallions
2 cloves garlic, mashed and chopped
1/2 teaspoon salt
1 1/2 teaspoons chopped parsley
1/2 teaspoon freshly ground white pepper
1/2 cup plain bread crumbs
a pinch of paprika

1. Cut the mirlitons in half and remove the seeds. In a large stockpot cover the mirlitons with water, bring to a boil, and cook over medium heat for 15 minutes, or until tender. Drain and let cool. When cool enough to handle, scoop the pulpy insides of the mirlitons into a bowl, reserving the shells.

2. In a large pot melt the butter over medium heat, add the ham and the onions, and cook for about 10 minutes, or until the onions soften. Stir in the chopped shrimp and the mirliton pulp, mashing if necessary. Add the scallions, garlic, salt, parsley, and white pepper, reduce the heat to a simmer, and cook for another 20 minutes.

3. Preheat the oven to 375 degrees. Add a bit more than half the bread crumbs to the pot to thicken the filling mixture and spoon the filling into the mirliton shells. In a small bowl mix the remaining bread crumbs with the pinch of paprika and sprinkle over the top of each stuffed mirliton. Bake for 15 minutes and serve warm.

Her smile is as wide and welcoming as her heart. Chef Leah Chase, lovingly known as the "Queen of Creole Cuisine," at an energetic 90 years old, represents the roots of what we do here. She is a beloved legend, cooking for such luminaries as the Rev. Martin Luther King, Jr., Duke Ellington, Thurgood Marshall, James Baldwin, Ray Charles, presidents, and just plain folks.

Before desegregation, it was a place for people of color. Today, race, creed or zip code doesn't matter a whit at Dooky Chase's. Leah and Dooky, her husband, founded one of the country's most culturally significant restaurants.

For her 90th birthday, the Edgar "Dooky" and Leah Chase Family Foundation was established to support social justice and the creative and culinary arts.

Leah has also been awarded the 2013 Ella Brennan Lifetime Achievement in Hospitality, presented by the New Orleans Wine and Food Experience. Leah and Ella are the city's culinary matriarchs, grand ladies, and icons.

Leah says that one should strive to make a person feel his or her worth, that this is a true measure of a person. "I had to get back on my feet," she told me following Katrina, "so I can start giving back." Leah, you never stopped.

Reprinted from The Dooky Chase Cookbook by Leah Chase, courtesy of Pelican Publishing Company.

Spanish settlers imported paella to New Orleans in the early 1700s and quickly adapted their recipes to make best use of the great available local ingredients they found here. Oysters and crawfish replaced clams and mussels. Andouille sausage replaced ham. And a new dish evolved. Certainly among the colony's earliest recipes, Jambalaya remains one of the most beloved and enduring.

Many dishes are named from mangled combinations of two or three languages. The newcomer was named jambon a la yaya. Jambon (ham) and à la (in the style of) being French. (Jamón is the Spanish word for ham.) And Yaya being the African word for rice, brought by slaves arriving in tandem with the Spanish settlers, then French settlers.

We continue to make jambalaya with whatever food and language is readily available. The most popular ingredients are chicken and sausage, or seafood, or a combination of them all.

(recipe continued from right)

duty pot) over medium heat. Add the chaurice and with a wooden spatula break it into small pieces. Raise the heat to medium high and add the andouille, ham, the chopped onion and celery, bell pepper, and Creole seasoning. Cook, stirring often, until the vegetables are browned, 15 to 20 minutes.

6. Add the rice and cook, stirring often, for 2 to 3 minutes, or until translucent. Add the shredded chicken, reserved broth, garlic, thyme, bay leaf, and 3/4 teaspoon of salt and bring to a boil. Reduce the heat to a simmer and cook, covered and undisturbed, for 20 to 25 minutes, or until the rice is just tender. Check the rice for doneness in several places. Remove the pot from the heat. Using a fork, gently fluff the scallions into the jambalaya. Cover and let stand for 10 minutes to let the flavors meld. Discard the bay leaf. Serve with the hot sauce, if you please.

POPPY TOOKER
CAJUN-STYLE CHICKEN *and* SAUSAGE JAMBALAYA

Louisiana-style ingredients are increasingly available these days, but it may be difficult to find the sausages and tasso. There are widely available substitutes (see the ingredient list below).

SERVES 8 to 10

a 2 1/2- to 3-pound chicken (giblets removed and reserved, if desired, for another use)
Kosher salt
freshly ground black pepper
1 large yellow onion, finely chopped, trimmings reserved
3 celery stalks, finely chopped, trimmings reserved
1 tablespoon canola oil
1/2 pound fresh chaurice or chorizo, casing removed
1/2 pound andouille or other smoked sausage, casing removed, halved lengthwise and cut into 1/4-inch segments
1/4 pound diced ham, preferably tasso
1 green bell pepper, stemmed, seeded, and finely chopped
1 teaspoon Creole seasoning
3 cups long-grain white rice
3 garlic cloves, minced
2 teaspoons chopped fresh thyme
1 dried bay leaf
1/2 cup thinly sliced scallions
Louisiana hot sauce to taste, if desired

1. Position a rack in the center of the oven and heat the oven to 325 degrees.

2. Pat the chicken dry and season it all over with salt and pepper. Put the chicken, breast side down, on a roasting rack in a medium (9- by 13-inch or similar) roasting pan or flameproof baking dish, and tuck the wing tips behind the neck.

3. Roast the chicken for 30 minutes. Turn it over and continue roasting about 45 minutes, or until an instant-read thermometer inserted in a thigh registers between 165 and 170 degrees. Transfer the chicken to a platter and let it rest until cool enough to handle, about 30 minutes. Pull off all the meat, discarding the skin and reserving the bones, into a bowl. Shred the meat into bite-size pieces, cover, and refrigerate.

4. Put the chicken bones in a 5- to 6-quart pot with the trimmings from the onion and celery. Add 8 cups of water and bring to a boil over high heat, skimming off any foam that rises to the surface. Lower the heat and simmer 35 to 50 minutes, or until flavorful and reduced to about 6 cups of liquid. Strain the broth into a bowl. You will need 6 cups, so measure the liquid and add water if necessary.

5. Heat the oil in a 7- to 8-quart enameled cast-iron Dutch oven (or other heavy-

(recipe continued at left)

BILLY WOHL
SEAFOOD GUMBO

When making a seafood gumbo, use fish or shellfish stock. For a chicken, turkey, and/or sausage gumbo, use chicken stock. It's all about the flavor, so please use stock rather than water. Just add shrimp shells or the chicken carcass, onion skins and celery tops to a stock pot (do not include bell pepper scraps). Cover with a gallon of water and boil for 20 minutes. Strain. Freeze any leftovers.

SERVES 6 to 8

4 tablespoons vegetable oil
4 tablespoons all-purpose flour
1 1/2 cups finely chopped celery
2 cups finely chopped onion
2 cups finely chopped stemmed and seeded green bell pepper
10 ounces frozen cut-up okra
4 tomatoes, diced (or a 16-ounce can, drained)
2 small cloves garlic, very finely chopped
1 1/2 teaspoons dried thyme
2 bay leaves
5 crabs, cleaned and quartered
2 quarts shrimp or fish stock
1/2 cup finely chopped parsley
1 teaspoon freshly ground black pepper
1/2 teaspoon cayenne pepper
1/2 cup finely chopped scallion
2 pounds peeled shrimp
3 to 4 cups cooked rice for serving

1. Using a heavy saucepan or cast iron skillet heat the oil over medium heat. Add the flour and cook, stirring frequently and being careful not to let the roux scorch, until it reaches the color of chocolate. This will take anywhere from 30 minutes up to an hour. Low and slow is the name of the game here. (See page 88 for complete instructions on how to make a roux).

2. Add the celery, onion, bell pepper, and okra and cook for about 10 minutes, stirring frequently, until softened. Stir in the tomatoes, garlic, thyme, bay leaves, crab quarters, and stock and cook over medium heat, stirring occasionally, for 10 minutes. Add the parsley, black pepper, and cayenne pepper and simmer for 30 to 45 minutes.

3. Stir in the scallion and shrimp and cook for another 10 minutes, or until the shrimp is cooked through. Serve warm over cooked rice.

Gumbo is one of those exemplary dishes that can be made in a number of ways and varies from cook to cook. My easy-going husband gets stubborn about his gumbo recipe. Yes, it's personal.

The emphasis is on the main ingredients: meat, poultry, seafood, or almost any combination of them all. Roux and the holy trinity of seasonings (celery, onion, and green bell peppers) create a smoky, dense taste—rich in texture and with hits of flavor.

Gumbo is always served over rice. In fact, with a salad and some hot French bread, there's no more satisfying meal. You may substitute any protein in any pleasing combination you desire.

Chef Greg Reggio began his career as an apprentice under the late, legendary Chef Warren LeRuth. He has great respect for the freshest and best products.

It is simple to create a splendid, beautiful redfish fillet that's flavorful on the outside and tenderly moist on the inside using his recipes and methods—a spectacular dish served for a buffet at room temperature.

One trick is to cool, then refrigerate, the covered fillets, then slice with a wet knife before service. The slices will hold together beautifully for presentation on a platter.

Greg is one of the Taste Buds, a trio of chefs who have developed ground-breaking restaurants and recipes at Zea Rotisserie and Semolina.

DILL SAUCE

MAKES a little more than 1 cup

2/3 cup fresh homemade mayonnaise
3 tablespoons fresh minced dill
1 tablespoon white vinegar
1 tablespoon Creole mustard
1/2 teaspoon dehydrated onion flakes
6 drops Tabasco hot sauce
2 tablespoons fresh-squeezed lemon juice

1. In a small mixing bowl, mix all the ingredients together well. Put in refrigerator for at least one hour to chill before serving.

CHEF GREG REGGIO, THE TASTE BUDS
REDFISH *on the* HALF SHELL

This recipe is one of our favorite company-is-coming recipes, especially for a crowd.

SERVES 4

four 1/2- to 3/4-inch-thick redfish fillets (about 6 ounces each)
4 teaspoons Seasoning Blend (see page 90)
4 teaspoons clarified unsalted butter or olive oil
4 tablespoons dill sauce

1. If using a gas grill, heat only one side of the grill. If using a charcoal grill, build a bank of coals along one side. Once the coals have burned down and are coated with ash, they will be ready.

2. Dust the skinless side of each fillet with a scant teaspoon of the Seasoning Blend and place it directly on the cool side of the grill.

3. Cover the grill and cook for 4 to 5 minutes. The fish will be done when the thickest part of the fillet is pressed with the tip of a finger and the impression remains. Alternately, gently flake the fish open: if the flesh is opaque, the fillet is done.

4. When the fillets are cooked, remove them from the grill and brush the skinless side of each with the clarified butter or olive oil.

5. Serve the redfish with the dill sauce ladled over the top or on the side.

CHEF TARIQ HANNA, SUCRÉ
KING CAKE

One of America's top-10 pastry chefs, Tariq Hanna of Sucré, has elevated the King Cake to rare beauty. Cream cheese and cinnamon are added to the buttery cake then pastel lustres shimmer their version, including baker's glazes and dusts. The specialty decorating items are available at craft stores and online. Otherwise, traditional King Cakes are decorated by pouring the white glaze over the cake, and sprinkling with colored sugars.

When did New Orleans get so silly over King Cake? We toss glittered shoes from floats and festoon trees with beads. And we eat King Cake. King Cake creativity has gone to extremes. If any rules apply (and here most don't), coloring almost anything edible with purple, green, and gold qualify it as King Cake.

SERVES 8 to 12

FOR THE DOUGH
2/3 cup whole milk,
    slightly above room temperature
1 1/2 teaspoons instant yeast
5 tablespoons sugar
1 teaspoon kosher salt
2 3/4 cups unbleached
    all-purpose flour
2 large eggs, room temperature
1 stick unsalted butter,
    cut into 1-inch pieces,
    plus 1/2 tablespoon, melted

FOR THE FILLING
8 ounces cream cheese
1 egg yolk
1/8 cup sugar
1 teaspoon vanilla extract
zest of 1 lemon

FOR THE CINNAMON SUGAR
1/2 cup sugar
1 tablespoon cinnamon

FOR THE GLAZE
2 cups confectioner's sugar
1/2 cup whole milk
1 teaspoon vanilla extract

Make the Dough

1. Mix the milk with the yeast in a large mixing bowl. In a separate mixing bowl, mix all the dry ingredients. Add the dry ingredients to the milk, kneading until they start to come together. Add the eggs one at a time, while continuing to knead. Add the melted butter and knead. Add the softened butter, one piece at a time, while continuing to knead until completely combined.

2. Place dough in a clean bowl and cover with plastic wrap. Keep at room temperature and allow dough to rise until it has doubled in size, usually 1 to 1 ½ hours.

3. Remove the plastic wrap and punch the dough back down with your hands. Cover with fresh plastic wrap and let rise until doubled, about 30 minutes.

Make the Filling

1. In a small mixing bowl, mix the cream cheese, egg yolk, sugar, vanilla extract, and lemon zest together until smooth.

Make the Cinnamon Sugar

1. In a small mixing bowl, combine the sugar and cinnamon thoroughly.

Assemble the Cake

1. Preheat oven to 360 degrees.

2. On a floured surface, roll the dough out into a rectangle about 10- by 14-inches. Cut the dough in half lengthwise to create two 5- by 14-inch strips.

3. Spoon the cream cheese filling onto the top 1/3 of each piece of dough, running the whole 14-inch length. Dust the whole piece with cinnamon sugar, using all of the mixture. Starting at the edges with the cream cheese filling, roll each piece into a log around the filling.

4. Overlap the logs carefully at one end and twist together to form a two-strand braid. Bring the two ends of the braid together to form an oval ring and press together to seal.

5. Gently place the ring seam-side down on a baking sheet lined with wax paper and cover with plastic wrap. Let it rise to double in size, about 30 minutes.

6. Bake for 20 to 25 minutes, or until golden brown. If the top has reached a golden brown before the bottom is finished, cover the top with foil and lower the heat to 325 degrees. Allow to cool.

Make the Glaze

1. Mix the sugar, milk, and vanilla extract together until smooth and divide into three small bowls. Color each separately with a drop of green, yellow, or purple (or combine red and blue) food colors.

2. Brush each glaze over the cooled cake and sprinkle with lustre dust. Serve the King Cake when the glaze has dried or keep covered until ready to serve.

King Cake babies are available on line, or use a dried bean or nut meat. Cut a slit in the bottom of the King Cake and insert the baby. Caution guests to take care biting down. Or, place the baby on top of the cake for everyone to admire.

Serve by slicing into 2-inch pieces.

FESTIVALS *and* FEAST DAYS

In New Orleans, and the rest of south Louisiana—as should be clear by now—we celebrate nearly everything.

The French Quarter Festival kicks off the festival season, as a four-day free music, and abundant food event. Every aspect of life in Louisiana has their special day. There are festivals dedicated to these and a thousand other foods, people, and events.

Just another excuse to exhibit our libertine ways?

Perhaps. Maybe that's what it looks like. But it's a richer story than that. The festivals that crowd the spring and fall calendars highlight and celebrate our vast and varied cultural and dining treasures. They are ways to give each and every item that comprises our broad palate the attention and honor they deserve.

And to bring a crowd of people together.

Of course, the mac-daddy of them all is the New Orleans Jazz and Heritage Festival at the New Orleans Fair Grounds racetrack. It's seven glorious, and hopefully sunny, days of the best music and food to be found in the region.

Jazz Fest, as locals call it, features dozens of outdoor food booths operated by select vendors from throughout the state, offering such dazzling and creative regional delicacies as stuffed crawfish bread, crawfish pasta, jambalaya, and gumbo.

It's a sweaty, intimate, communal feast. Don't be alarmed if someone hovers too close to your dish; they just want to know what you're eating. Don't even be surprised if a stranger not only informs you of the ingredients and quality of his or her own selection, but also holds out their fork to offer you a taste.

Such is the Louisiana way. Nowhere is food honored so reverently, publicly, ubiquitously. Festivals are the pride of small towns across south Louisiana—celebrations thrown open to all comers for a taste of the great Louisiana outdoors.

THE TASTE BUDS, ZEA ROTISSERIE & GRILL
SPINACH SALAD

Zea's spinach salad was the winner in a culinary competition a few years ago. Chef Greg Reggio, one of the Taste Buds, remembered the commitment at the last minute and quickly put together the ingredients he had on hand for his entry. It was a hit then and continues to be the restaurant's most popular salad. Zea also bottles and sells their own special vinaigrette for the salad, while the following recipe for it is an approximation.

SERVES 4 to 8

FOR THE PEPPER JELLY VINAIGRETTE
1/2 cup pepper jelly
4 tablespoons balsamic vinegar
1 teaspoon garlic powder
1 teaspoon kosher salt
1 cup olive oil

FOR THE SALAD
12 ounces baby spinach
1 teaspoon sesame seeds
4 tablespoons sun-dried tomatoes
4 tablespoons golden raisins
4 tablespoons roasted pecans
8 Kalamata olives
1/2 cup crumbled blue cheese

Make the Pepper Jelly Vinaigrette

1. Whisk together the pepper jelly, balsamic vinegar, garlic powder, and salt, making sure to break up any clumps of garlic powder or salt.

2. Gradually add the oil in a slow, steady stream, whisking constantly until blended.

Make the Salad

1. Wash the spinach, drain well, and place in a large serving bowl.

2. Top with all the other dry ingredients. Pour the vinaigrette over the salad, toss, and serve immediately.

BARRY GARNER
STRAWBERRY SPINACH SALAD

Production chief Barry Garner came to New Orleans from the Pacific Northwest to attend to Tulane University and no one has yet been able to convince him to leave. Arriving with enough culinary aptitude to feed himself, Barry has picked up enough expertise working here to unabashedly serve meals to guests.

Ponchatoula's annual Strawberry Festival has been drawing New Orleanians across Lake Pontchartrain to every second weekend of April since 1972. The festival hosts a parade, pageants, music, rides, and, of course, food. With standard festival foods like funnel cake, the Strawberry Festival provides a Louisiana twist with treats like gator and fresh Louisiana strawberries. Available by themselves, deep-fried in batter, in pies, sauces, daiquiris, beer, as jam and jelly, and any other way you can imagine using them, Louisiana strawberries are truly the star of the show.

SERVES 8

juice of 1 large lemon
1/4 cup sugar
1 egg yolk, whisked
6 tablespoons vegetable oil
2 bunches fresh spinach leaves, washed well
1 pint strawberries, stemmed and halved or quartered

1. In a medium mixing bowl, stir the lemon juice and sugar together and whisk in the egg yolk.

2. Add the vegetable oil to the mixture, 1 tablespoon at a time, whisking well between each addition.

3. Toss the strawberries and spinach in a serving bowl with the dressing and serve slightly chilled.

A year of frolic

ARCHIE CASBARIAN, REMOULADE
MEAT PIES

Arnaud's casual café, Remoulade, around the corner on Bourbon Street, serves a continuous food festival year round. Meat pies from South Louisiana are a tradition brought to the forefront via Jazz Fest food vendors, another savory favorite that may be seasoned to taste.

MAKES 12

1 pound spicy pork breakfast sausage, or 1/2 pound sausage and 1/2 pound ground beef
1 medium onion, finely diced
1/2 medium red bell pepper, finely diced
2 cloves garlic, minced
1 small Louisiana yam (or sweet potato), peeled and coarsely grated
1 teaspoon chopped fresh basil
1/4 teaspoon cayenne pepper
1/4 teaspoon cracked black pepper
1/4 teaspoon white pepper
2 teaspoons Worcestershire sauce
1/2 cup Cheddar cheese, grated
3 sheets puff pastry, 9- by 9-inches, from the grocery freezer section
1 egg beaten with 1 tablespoon of water for egg wash

To make the pies

1. Remove the puff pastry from the freezer to thaw. Do not microwave it. Preheat the oven to 375 degrees.

2. In a large skillet over medium heat, sauté the meat. Using a spatula, crumble it into small pieces as it cooks. Remove from pan and drain on paper towels once cooked.

3. Keeping 1 tablespoon of the fat from the meat in the pan, add the onion, bell pepper, and garlic. Cook until soft. Add the grated yam and cook 10 to 15 minutes. Add the basil, the peppers, and Worcestershire sauce. Add the cheese. Return the meat to the pan and mix thoroughly. Remove from heat.

4. On a lightly floured surface, roll out the puff pastry to about 1/8-inch thick. Using a 4-inch plate as a guide, cut out 4 circles of pastry from each of the three sheets. Place the circles on parchment paper—lined baking sheets.

5. Place a heaping tablespoon of the filling off center of each pastry circle. Brush egg wash around the outer edge of each circle and fold each circle in half, enclosing the dough.

6. Press the outer edge of the now half-circles of pastry with either your fingers or the tines of a fork to close them securely. Brush each pie lightly with egg wash and bake for 30 to 35 minutes.

(recipe continued at right)

Brother and sister, Archie and Katy Casbarian, are this generation's proprietors of Arnaud's and Remoulade in the best restaurant family dynasty tradition we embrace.

(recipe continued from left)

7. Once the pies have turned golden brown, remove them from the oven and let cool 5 to 10 minutes. Serve warm.

Music and food festivals—joyous madness—we agonize over which musicians are on the personal must-hear list, then debate food booths not to be missed. It's a schedule deserving of attention ... and sometimes compromise.

What are the proper accouterments for outdoor events? Most certainly, hats wearing flowers, feathers, and/or ribbons. Who can dance without an umbrella, the fanciful one last used, probably, for a second-line?

Decorated flag poles are also to be carried. Those, too, are left to the imagination, but may not be made of metal and must be lightweight enough to be carried high, to avoid blocking sight lines.

The rule of thumb is to dress, eat, dance, and decorate more with abandon than design.

Jyl Benson is an acclaimed foodie and successful author of cookbooks and creative recipes.

JYL BENSON
STUFFED CRAWFISH BREAD

Crawfish tails are cooked with cheese, butter, and seasonings, then baked in bread. Think of it as finger food. Whenever and wherever it is served, it's a festival.

SERVES 12

1/4 cup butter, plus 3 tablespoons melted for brushing the tops
2 cups finely chopped onion
1 cup finely chopped green bell pepper
2 tablespoons minced garlic
1 pound peeled Louisiana crawfish tails with fat
1/4 cup chopped scallions
1 tablespoon hot sauce
1/2 teaspoon salt
1/2 teaspoon freshly ground black pepper
a 48-ounce package frozen bread dough, defrosted
1 1/2 cups shredded mozzarella or Monterey Jack cheese
1 1/2 cups shredded Cheddar cheese

1. Preheat the oven to 350 degrees.

2. In a large skillet over medium-high heat, melt 1/4 cup butter. Add the onion and sauté over medium heat for 5 to 10 minutes, or until translucent. Add the bell pepper and garlic and sauté for 5 to 8 minutes. Add the crawfish, scallions, hot sauce, and salt and pepper and cook another 5 minutes to allow the flavors to marry. Cover, remove from heat, and set aside.

3. On a lightly floured surface, roll each defrosted bread-dough roll out into a 20- by 5-inch rectangle. Cut each rectangle in half width-wise to make six 10- by 5-inch rectangles. Spoon about 1/2 cup of the crawfish mixture slightly off center on each piece of dough. Top the crawfish mixture with 1/4 cup of each type of cheese. Fold the dough over and pinch the edges together to seal. Cut 2-inch slits in the top of the filled dough for venting.

4. Place the loaves on a greased baking sheet and brush the tops with melted butter. Bake for 25 to 30 minutes. Slice and serve warm.

THE TASTE BUDS
JAZZY CRAWFISH ROBAN

This creamy, crawfish-studded type of pasta recipe is a Jazz Fest favorite—a festival of flavors dancing on the same plate. Fresh shrimp or crab meat may be substituted for fresh crawfish tails.

SERVES 6

FOR THE SAUCE
1/4 cup unsalted butter
1/4 cup minced garlic
1 cup finely chopped scallions
1 quart heavy whipping cream
1 tablespoon blackened redfish seasoning (see page 90)
salt and freshly ground white pepper to taste

1 1/2 pounds pasta shells
1 pound Louisiana crawfish tails, preferably fresh
1/4 cup finely chopped scallions
1 cup grated Parmigiano-Reggiano

Make the Sauce

1. Melt the butter in a 12-inch or larger heavy-bottomed saucepan, add the garlic and scallions, and cook over medium heat until the garlic releases its flavor, about 3 minutes.

2. Stir in the heavy cream and reduce the heat to low. Cook until reduced by half, stirring frequently, about 20 to 30 minutes. The sauce is the proper consistency when it is thick enough to heavily coat the back of a spoon. Add the blackened redfish seasoning and salt and pepper to taste. Reduce the heat and keep warm.

Cook the pasta according to the directions on the package, drain, and place in a large serving bowl. Drain any liquid from the crawfish tails and add them to the sauce. Return the sauce to a simmer and cook for 5 minutes. Pour the sauce over the pasta and toss to coat the pasta well. Fold in the Parmigiano-Reggiano and sprinkle with the scallions.

The Taste Buds named this recipe for Lionel Robin, a Louisiana chef from Henderson, just east of Breaux Bridge. His name is pronounced "Roban," but naming a dish after him was a challenge as people tended to say it like the bird—hence the creative spelling.

The Taste Buds are a trio of chefs with ground-breaking restaurants. Chefs Gary Darling, Hans Limburg, and Greg Reggio gave themselves the name of The Taste Buds, and their business took off like crazy, devising outrageous dishes to match their personalities, prepared à la minute—at the last minute. Their concepts include Semolina, Zea Rotisserie, and more to come.

P&J Oysters, the county's oldest business of its kind in the United States, has been cultivating and harvesting oysters for more than 130 years. Sal Sunseri, a member of the family owned and operated company, helped to found the annual New Orleans Oyster Festival, occurring early each summer.

Chef Stephen Stryjewski, prior to opening Cochon, worked with his now partner Donald Link at Herbsaint Restaurant. Cochon has expanded to include The Butcher, and the S'wine Bar.

The restaurant was nominated in its first year as a James Beard Foundation Best New Restaurant, South. Stephen was awarded the Foundation's Best Chef, Southeast, in 2011.

CHEF STEPHEN STRYJEWSKI, COCHON

GRILLED OYSTERS *with* GARLIC-CHILI BUTTER

Cochon's wood-burning oven quickly roasts this specialty. The oysters are also successfully cooked on a grill (preferably charcoal) or under the oven broiler. And yes, there is no cheese in the recipe.

MAKES 32 grilled oysters

6 garlic cloves
4 anchovy fillets
2 lemons, zested and juiced
1 pound (4 sticks) unsalted butter, cut into cubes, at room temperature
4 tablespoons garlic chili paste
4 teaspoons crushed red pepper flakes
1/2 teaspoon cayenne pepper
2 teaspoons salt
32 freshly shucked oysters on the half shell
lemon wedges for garnish

1. Mince the garlic, anchovies, and lemon zest, place in a medium-sized bowl, and fold in the lemon juice, butter, garlic chile paste, red pepper flakes, cayenne, and salt.

2. Turn the garlic-chile butter out onto a sheet of plastic wrap and mold into a log about 1 1/2 inches in diameter. Roll the log in the plastic wrap and refrigerate 30 minutes, or until chilled through. (The butter mixture should be made as fresh as possible.)

3. Preheat the grill to high. Place the oysters on a heatproof serving tray. Cut 1/4-inch slices of the garlic-chile butter and place one on each oyster. Using tongs, place the oysters on the grill for 6 to 10 minutes, or until the oysters begin to bubble and the edges curl up. Return the oysters carefully with the tongs to the serving tray and serve immediately with the lemon wedges as garnish. Offer warm French bread for dipping.

BOYSIE BOLLINGER, BOLLINGER SHIPYARDS
BOYSIE'S EGGPLANT SHRIMP SUPREME

Shrimp and eggplant casserole is a Bollinger friends and family favorite that also freezes beautifully. Spicy delicious if you prefer, or simply use non-spicy sausage.

SERVES 10 to 12

2 large yellow onions
1 large green bell pepper
1/2 stalk celery
10-ounce can Ro-Tel original tomatoes
2 medium eggplants
1 pound Jimmy Dean Breakfast Sausage
1 pint sliced mushrooms
1 pound medium peeled shrimp
1/4 cup Italian bread crumbs
1 tablespoon Italian seasoning
Creole seasoning to taste

1. Chop the onions, bell pepper, and celery and place in a large heavy pot. Add the tomatoes and cover. Let simmer on low heat while preparing the rest of the ingredients.

2. Peel the eggplants and cut into 1/2-inch cubes. Cover with water in a medium-sized pot and simmer until soft, about 30 minutes. Drain and set aside.

3. Cook the sausage in a large skillet until dark brown. Drain the fat and add to the simmering vegetables along with the cooked eggplant, mushrooms, and shrimp. Continue cooking until the mushrooms darken, about 30 minutes.

4. Add the Italian seasoning, bread crumbs, and Creole seasoning. Simmer another 15 minutes and serve warm.

ysha H Jordan

Louisiana's Bollinger Shipyards builds much larger crafts, but none the less important. Chairman Boysie Bollinger is well known as an avid hunter and fisherman, happily chopping and sautéing his catch in the midst of community and civic activities.

The annual Blessing of the Fleet ushers in seafood's many seasons, providing a sense of community and well-being. Small marinas across the state hold their own ceremonies for blessings, with fancifully dressed boats to parade with kings and queens. Our blessing is seafood so fresh it almost lands on your plate without an assist.

It's a special and rare treat to buy seafood directly from the boat. Produced by the hard-working Delcambre, Louisiana families, the website delcambredirectseafood.com provides links to the fishermen and their dockside schedules. It doesn't get any fresher unless you're fishing with Boysie.

Devotees cheered when Hubig's fried pies returned home after Hurricane Katrina. The hand-sized pastries, each wrapped in waxy paper, signaled that all would again be right with our world. A fire destroyed the plant, shuttering it again in the summer of 2012, but rebuilding is promised.

Joe Truill fried pies as the pastry chef at NOLA, Emeril Lagasse's French Quarter restaurant. A decade there and thousands of pies—could be more—later have made him a master. Chefs Joe and Heidi Truill continue to fry pies at Grits & Groceries—their Belton, South Carolina, restaurant.

(recipe continued from right)

2. Coat the edge of each circle of dough with the egg wash. Place 2 tablespoons of the fruit mixture in the center of each circle, fold the dough over to form a closed half-circle, and crimp the edges firmly shut with your fingers or the tines of a fork.

3. In a deep-fat fryer or a pan on the stovetop, heat the oil to 350 degrees. Gently slide the pies, a few at a time, into the oil, leaving enough room for them to float freely. Cook for about 8 to 10 minutes, or until the dough is crisp and lightly browned. Transfer with a slotted spoon to crumpled newspaper or paper towels or to a rack set over a baking sheet. Allow to cool slightly.

Make the Sugar Coating

1. Mix the sugar and orange zest in a small bowl.

2. Place the pies, one at a time, in the sugar mixture and toss gently to coat completely.

Serve the pies plain, or gild the lily with ice cream.

CHEF JOE TRULL, GRITS & GROCERIES
FRIED FRUIT PIES

Filled with fresh fruit, these home-fried pies are made with a dough a little softer than standard piecrust and which is sealed by crimping all the way around.

SERVES 10

FOR THE FILLING
4 cups trimmed and chopped fresh fruit
1 cup sugar
1 teaspoon chopped orange zest
1 tablespoon fresh orange juice
2 teaspoons vanilla extract
3 tablespoons cornstarch
1 tablespoon butter
1/2 teaspoon salt

FOR THE DOUGH
4 cups all-purpose flour
2 1/2 teaspoons Kosher salt
1 cup vegetable shortening or high-quality lard
an egg wash, made by beating 1 egg with 1 teaspoon of water

2 quarts oil for frying

FOR THE SUGAR COATING
2 cups sugar
3 teaspoons orange zest

Make the Filling

1. In a medium sized mixing bowl combine the fruit, sugar, orange zest, orange juice, and vanilla. Mix gently and chill, covered, for at least 6 hours, preferably overnight.

2. In a large saucepan bring the fruit mixture to a boil, reduce the heat, and simmer for about 5 minutes, or until it is tender. While the fruit is cooking, combine the cornstarch with 2 teaspoons of water in a small bowl. Add the cornstarch mixture, butter, and salt to the pan and cook another 7 to 10 minutes, or until a jam-like consistency is reached. Remove from the heat and allow to cool.

Make the Dough

1. In another mixing bowl, combine the flour and salt. Knead the shortening or lard into the dry ingredients until the mixture resembles a course meal. Add 3/4 to 1 cup water, a 1/4 cup at a time, until the dough comes together but is not sticky.

2. Shape the dough into a disk, wrap it in plastic wrap, and chill for at least an hour.

Make the Fruit Pies

1. On a floured surface roll half of the dough out to about 1/8 inch thick. Using a round cutter, 6 inches across, cut out circles of dough. Form the scraps into a ball, reroll, and cut out more circles. The dough should yield ten circles.

(recipe continued on left)

CHEF MICHELLE McRANEY, MR. B'S BISTRO
POTATO LEEK SOUP

This delicately balanced, hearty soup is simple to prepare. There's no need to wait for St. Patrick's Day.

SERVES 6 to 8

4 cups peeled and diced potatoes
3 cups well washed, thinly sliced leeks
salt and freshly ground black pepper to taste
6 tablespoons heavy cream
2 tablespoons minced chives

1. In a 4-quart saucepan simmer the potatoes and leeks in 2 quarts of water, partially covered, until soft, about 40 minutes.

2. Pass the potato leek mixture through a food mill or purée in a blender. Add salt and pepper to taste.

3. When ready to serve, bring the soup back to a simmer. Remove from heat, stir in the cream, and top each serving with minced chives.

Mr. B's stands for Brennan's, another mighty offshoot of the restaurant group—the Commander's Palace side of the family, if you're keeping score.

Managing Partner, Cindy Brennan, works closely with Executive Chef, Michelle McRaney, to provide Creole-style specialties in the French Quarter.

Since the Brennan family is very proud of their Irish heritage, St. Patrick's Day is an important day of celebration at their multitude of restaurants. The Brennan clan, of course, is another of our famous restaurant family dynasties.

CHEF MICHELLE McRANEY, MR. B'S BISTRO
CORNED BEEF *and* CABBAGE

The first St. Patrick's Day in New Orleans was celebrated in 1809. The city, never one to pass up the opportunity to have a good time, quickly adapted the celebration to suit the environment. Multiple parades run for St. Patricks day now—in the French Quarter, the Irish Channel, and the suburbs. While modeled somewhat after the Mardi Gras parades, the throws are a bit different, including cabbage, potatoes, and anything else needed for a good Irish stew. Because we know you can't have a celebration without the right food. Eli Sanders, at left, caught his lucky cabbage.

SERVES 6 to 8

two 2 1/2-pound corned beef briskets
1 tablespoon coarsely ground black pepper
1 teaspoon allspice
2 bay leaves
2 teaspoons Kosher salt
1/2 pound diced carrots
1/2 pound diced onions
1 pound peeled and diced potatoes
1/2 pound diced celery
1 small cabbage, diced

1. Place the corned beef, black pepper, allspice, bay leaves, and salt in a large pot and cover with 3 quarts of water. Cover and bring the mixture to a boil. Reduce the heat to low and cook at a low simmer for 2 1/2 hours.

2. Add the carrots, onions, potatoes, and celery, and cook, uncovered, for 15 to 20 minutes. Add the cabbage and cook for another 15 to 20 minutes.

3. Serve the corned beef and cabbage hot, divided among large soup bowls.

New Orleans has always been a melting pot of a multi-cultural city, and the Irish began to arrive in the late 1700s. They were able to get cheap passage on cargo ships that unloaded their cotton in Liverpool and needed ballast for their return journey.

The Catholic history of the city also provided a more familiar environment for many as opposed to the predominantly Protestant cities elsewhere in the country. Looking for jobs, the Irish settled upriver of the downtown area along the banks of the Mississippi, where they could find work unloading the same ships that originally brought them here.

This area, while no longer ethnically Irish, is still referred to as the Irish Channel, and their mark remains in the form of several of the churches the early arrivals built, such as St. Alphonsus.

CHEF MICHELLE McRANEY, MR. B'S BISTRO
IRISH CREAM CHEESECAKE

A deliciously smooth and appropriately flavored cheese cake.

SERVES 8

FOR THE CRUST
1 cup graham cracker crumbs
3 tablespoons white sugar
2 tablespoons unsalted butter, melted

FOR THE CHEESECAKE
three 8-ounce packages cream cheese
1 cup white sugar
2 teaspoons vanilla extract
1 cup sour cream
1/2 cup Bailey's Irish Cream
4 eggs

FOR THE ICING
1 cup sour cream
1/4 cup white sugar

Make the Crust

1. Preheat the oven to 350 degrees.

2. In a medium mixing bowl mix together the graham cracker crumbs and sugar thoroughly, and stir in the melted butter. Press the crust mixture into the bottom of a 9-inch springform pan.

3. Bake the crust until browned, about 8 minutes. Set aside, leaving the oven on.

Make the Cheesecake

1. Using an electric mixer, beat the cream cheese, sugar, and vanilla in a large bowl until blended. Add the sour cream and the Bailey's and beat in the eggs, one at a time, until the mixture is just combined.

2. Pour the mixture on top of the crust. Return cheesecake to the oven and bake until the edges are puffed and the center is firm, about 1 1/2 hours. Remove from oven (keep oven heated) and cool for 15 to 20 minutes.

Make the Icing

1. While the cheesecake is cooling, mix the sour cream and sugar together in a small bowl until smooth. Spread the icing evenly over the top of the cooled cake and

(recipe continued at right)

"Kiss me, I'm Irish," is the old saying. During St. Patrick's Day events, revelers trade carnations for a quick smooch. There's a whole lot of kissing going on. Pretty girls get lots of flowers.

Those unfortunates not wearing green in public on St. Patrick's Day risk getting a pinch instead.

(recipe continued from left)

bake the cheesecake for 10 minutes more.

2. Allow the cheesecake to cool on a baker's rack, cover it loosely with plastic wrap, and refrigerate overnight.

The days leading up to St. Joseph's are when many Italian families construct elaborate homemade altars in their homes to honor their particular patron saint. These displays—bountiful, intricate, and ornate offerings of breads, meats, sweets, and candies—could feed whole neighborhoods. And often do.

Stuffed artichokes are labor intensive with a heavenly flavor well worth the effort. They freeze well. Re-heat by steaming them over water. Someone's grandma makes these, especially during the Italian Festival celebrated around St. Joseph's day. They were grown on the West Bank as early as 1751 just across the river from Jackson Square in Algiers Point by Jean Charles Pradel, a small planter, merchant, and former French military officer.

FRANKY & JOHNNY'S
STUFFED ARTICHOKES

Franky & Johnny's, a now-closed neighborhood seafood joint served these as a feature.

SERVES 12 to 18

6 large artichokes
5 lemons
10 cups Italian seasoned breadcrumbs
1 1/2 cups Parmigiano-Reggiano cheese or 1 1/2 cups good domestic parmesan, grated
1 1/2 cups Pecorino Romano cheese, grated
1 cup scallions, chopped
1/2 cup parsley, chopped
12 garlic cloves, finely minced
2 tablespoons salt
1 tablespoon freshly ground black pepper
1 tablespoon cayenne pepper
2 1/2 to 3 cups olive oil
6 lemon slices

1. Using scissors, trim off the pointed ends of each artichoke and rub a lemon on the cut ends to prevent browning. Slice off the stem ends so the artichokes stand up straight.

2. Combine all the ingredients, except the artichokes, in a large bowl and mix stuffing well.

3. Spread the leaves of each artichoke open, without breaking them, and tuck as much stuffing as possible down into each leaf, tapping the artichoke gently to let any loose stuffing fall off.

4. Stand the artichokes in a casserole or roasting pan just large enough to hold them in a single layer. Add water to a depth of 1 1/2 inches and pour a generous amount of olive oil over each artichoke, letting it seep in. Top each artichoke with a slice of lemon.

5. Bring the water to a boil, reduce the heat to low, and steam the artichokes, covered and checking occasionally to see if necessary to add more water, for 45 minutes to an hour (possibly more), or until the leaves pull away easily and the pith is soft. Serve hot or warm.

Optional: Add 1 cup fried chopped bacon or pancetta to stuffing mixture.

The stuffed artichokes can be prepared in advance and reheated before serving. Leftover stuffing keeps for 2 weeks in the refrigerator and longer in the freezer.

CHEF MARY JO MOSCA, MOSCA'S
CHICKEN *à la* GRANDE

Not much has changed since Provino and Lisa Mosca opened Mosca's Restaurant in 1946 in a white clapboard road house out on Highway 90 across the river. Between 1946 and 1947, before the Kefauver Commission shut it down, gambling here was widespread. After leaving local gaming houses such as Old Southport, the Beverly, Club Forrest, and O'Dwyer's, patrons would come to Mosca's for a late-night post-gambling meal.

Perhaps because of those particular guests, Mosca's does not accept credit cards or checks. Cash only. Now they also close early evening.

SERVES 4

a 3-pound chicken, cut into eighths
3/4 cup olive oil
1 tablespoon salt
1 tablespoon freshly ground black pepper
6-10 cloves peeled garlic, pounded
1 tablespoon dried rosemary
1 tablespoon oregano
1/2 cup dry white wine, like chardonnay

1. Place the chicken in a skillet with the olive oil and turn to coat completely. Season evenly with salt and pepper.

2. Turn the heat on to medium. Cook for about 25 minutes to brown the chicken on all sides, turning as needed.

3. Add the garlic, rosemary, and oregano, and stir to make sure the chicken pieces are coated evenly. Reduce heat to low and add the wine. Simmer until the wine has reduced by about half, another 10-15 minutes. Serve immediately with the pan juices.

While the first Italian in Lousiana, Henry de Tonti, arrived with one of the earliest expeditions, the Italians did not show up in large numbers until the 1880s. These immigrants were mostly from Sicily. The St. Joseph's Day altars give thanks for relief from a devestating Sicilian famine.

The Italian American Marching Club in New Orleans was founded in 1970 and has grown to over 1,500 members in recent years. Founded by Joseph Cardenia, the club celebrates the heritage and contributions of New Orleans' Italian-American population and, of course, parades.

Each year they step out into the French Quarter around St. Joseph's day in tuxedoes and gowns to throw beads and bestow garters on the chosen few. Of course, royalty ride the floats, and gentlemen trade carnations for kisses.

The James Beard Foundation named Emeril Lagasse as the recipient of its 2013 Humanitarian of the Year Award. His foundation has raised $5.3 million for children's education and culinary arts.

(recipe continued from right)

to the dry mixture and combine to make a rough dough.

2. Turn the dough out onto a lightly floured surface and knead until smooth, about 5 minutes. Cut the dough into 4 pieces, wrap each piece in plastic wrap, and refrigerate for 45 minutes.

3. Preheat the oven to 375. Lightly grease 2 large baking sheets. On a lightly floured surface, roll out the dough, one piece at a time, into a 12-inch square. Cut the dough into 4- by 3-inch rectangles.

4. Spoon 2 tablespoons of filling down the center of each rectangle. Fold the long sides of each rectangle inward to the center to enclose the filling and pinch the edges together firmly to seal. Turn the cookies seam-sides down and press gently to flatten the seams.

5. With a floured knife, cut the logs crosswise into 1 1/2-inch-wide slices and arrange the slices 1/2 inch apart on the prepared baking sheets. Brush the tops with the egg wash and decorate with the colored sprinkles.

6. Bake until golden brown, about 20 minutes, transfer to wire racks to cool, and serve warm or at room temperature.

This recipe by Emeril Lagasse originally appeared Emeril Live on Food Network, courtesy Martha Stewart Living OmniMedia, Inc.

CHEF EMERIL LAGASSE, EMERIL'S
ITALIAN FIG COOKIES

It wouldn't be fitting to have a St. Joseph's Day alter without these special cookies, a prayer and a lucky bean to sustain petitioners in the coming year. The Lucky Bean is a token of properity, good luck and promise of bountiful blessings.

MAKES about 4 dozen

FOR THE FILLING
2 cups dried figs, hard tips discarded
1 1/2 cups dried dates, pitted
1 cup raisins
3/4 cup whole almonds, toasted and coarsely chopped
3/4 cup whole walnuts, toasted and coarsely chopped
1/2 cup orange marmalade
1/2 cup honey
1/4 cup brandy
1 teaspoon finely grated fresh orange zest
1 teaspoon finely grated fresh lemon zest
1 teaspoon ground cinnamon
1/2 teaspoon freshly grated nutmeg
1/4 teaspoon ground cloves

FOR THE DOUGH
4 cups all-purpose flour
3/4 cup sugar
1 tablespoon plus 1 teaspoon baking powder
1/2 teaspoon salt
2 sticks (1 cup) butter, cut into 1/2-inch cubes
1 large egg
1/2 cup milk
1 tablespoon vanilla
1 egg white beaten with 1 tablespoon water to make an egg wash
colored sprinkles for decoration

Make the Filling

1. In a food processor, finely chop the figs, dates, and raisins.

2. Transfer the mixture to a medium bowl, add the remaining filling ingredients, and stir to combine well. Cover and refrigerate for at least 8 hours.

Make the Dough

1. In a large bowl combine the flour, sugar, baking powder, and salt and whisk to combine well. Add the butter and blend with your fingertips until most of mixture resembles coarse meal.

In a medium bowl, beat the egg, milk, and vanilla together. Add the wet mixture

(recipe continued at left)

HAUNTS, GRIS GRIS *and* GHOULIES

In most places, Halloween is all about children—their costumes, revelry, and, of course, treats. And sure, New Orleans has that.

But why waste a perfectly fine opportunity for adults to masquerade once again, costuming being such a rich tradition in the city. Most New Orleanians have in their homes a "Mardi Gras closet," a storage area reserved just for costumes and accessories from which they can muster up a proper outfit for themselves and guests on a minute's notice.

The supernatural is a prevailing element of New Orleans culture. Our cemeteries are tourist sites, ghost and vampire tours clog French Quarter sidewalks at night, and, of course, voodoo shops ply their wares of potions, candles, potpourri, gris-gris sacks, and the other amenities of the tradition.

Kidney beans, candies, cigars, and fine liquors are common offerings found at the bases of various cemetery tombs where voodoo queens, mystics, and healers are believed to be buried.

Even the other-worldly spirits of New Orleans partake of the daily feast that is life in this lush, mysterious, and Gothic city. New Orleans is universally considered the most haunted city in America.

And it is well established that its meals are hauntingly good, heavenly rich, and devilishly delightful.

The novice diner has a more than a ghost of a chance to eat their way through the rich bounty of the autumn harvest—hunt and catch.

When Toups' Meatery opened in 2012, you weren't paying attention if you weren't excited. Husband and wife owners, Chef Isaac and Amanda Toups have been in New Orleans food for years. Chef Toups worked his way up through Emeril's organization before being named the Times-Picayune's Chef to Watch in 2010. Almost everything on the menu is meant to share.

On special occasions, the streets belong to the mysterious and rowdy Indian tribes, gangs of largely middle-class African Americans, who dress out in spectacular Native American suits of rhinestone, beads, plumes, and sequins.

The secretive groups—with their rigid hierarchies of spy boys, flag boys, chiefs, and wild men—stalk each other through downtown neighborhoods, taunting each other with chants of bravado, out-drumming and out-dancing each other and concluding each "battle" with robust arguments over whose outfits are "most pretty."

Not something you'll likely encounter on your next visit to any other otherworldly place.

CHEF ISAAC TOUPS, TOUPS' MEATERY
DEVILED EGGS *with* GHOST CAVIAR

Ghost caviar is roe from the prehistoric choupiquet fish, infused with ghost pepper, supposedly the world's hottest chili pepper. The tiny Cajun Caviar Company produces several varieties of the Louisiana delicacy, which ranks among the finest Malossol caviars in the world. It is available at www.cajuncaviar.com.

MAKES 2 dozen deviled eggs

1 dozen eggs
4 tablespoons Louisiana hot sauce
2 tablespoons Worcestershire sauce
5 tablespoons mayonnaise
5 tablespoons horseradish
2 tablespoons Creole mustard
1/4 teaspoon wasabi powder
24 slices pickled jalapeño
2 slices cooked bacon, broken up for garnish
3 ounces caviar

1. In a large saucepan, cover the eggs with water by about an inch and bring to a boil over medium heat. When a boil is reached, remove the pan from the heat and let stand for 15 minutes. Crack the shells of the eggs as you transfer them to a bowl of ice water (this makes them much easier to peel). Chill the eggs for 10 minutes and peel them very carefully to avoid damaging the whites.

2. Cut each egg in half with a very sharp knife. Scoop the yolks into a food processor and place the whites gently in a large mixing bowl. In a small bowl, mix 2 tablespoons of the hot sauce with the Worcestershire sauce and pour over the egg whites. Very gently mix the egg whites with the hot sauce mixture so they are completely coated. Let the eggs stand for 10 minutes and carefully drain off any excess. Arrange the whites, cut sides up, on a serving plate.

3. Add the other 2 tablespoons of hot sauce, mayonnaise, horseradish, Creole mustard, and wasabi powder to the egg yolks in the food processor and blend until smooth.

4. Pipe an equal amount of the yolk mixture into each of the egg whites, top with a slice of pickled jalapeño and piece of bacon, and garnish with caviar.

CHEF TOM COWMAN, RESTAURANT JONATHAN
ANGELS ON HORSEBACK

This recipe was among scores of classic recipes Chef Tom Cowman created.

SERVES 4

FOR THE MAITRE d'HÔTEL BUTTER
3 cups (6 sticks) softened butter
3 tablespoons minced scallion
2 tablespoons chopped fresh basil
4 tablespoons chopped fresh chives
2 tablespoons chopped parsley
2 tablespoons chopped fresh chervil
1 tablespoon onion powder
1 garlic clove, minced
Worcestershire sauce to taste
Louisiana hot sauce to taste
1 tablespoons fresh lemon juice

FOR THE FRIED OYSTERS
12 slices of bacon
24 shucked fresh oysters
4 slices soft white bread
vegetable oil for frying
1 cup rice flour
4 lemon wedges for garnish
4 parsley sprigs for garnish

Make the Maitre d'Hôtel Butter

Heat all the ingredients in a medium sauce pan until warmed through.

Prepare the Fried Oysters

1. Cut the slices of bacon in half. Bring a medium pot of water to a boil and parboil the bacon for about 10 minutes, or until it curls. Drain the bacon and let cool until it can be handled. Wrap each oyster with a half strip of bacon, secure with a toothpick, and refrigerate.

2. Preheat the oven to 350 degrees. Cut a 3-inch round from each slice of bread and brush each round liberally with the Maitre d'Hôtel Butter. Transfer the rounds to a baking sheet and bake until golden brown, about 5 minutes. Transfer the rounds to separate plates and keep warm.

3. Heat the oil in a Dutch oven or electric deep-fryer to 350 degrees. Roll the bacon-wrapped oysters in the rice flour to coat. Using tongs, transfer the oysters

(recipe continued at right)

The late, much-beloved Tom Cowman made headlines when he was chef at Restaurant Jonathan in New Orleans during the late 1970s. After that Art-Deco style establishment closed in 1986, he moved to the Upperline restaurant.

A stunning portrait by artist Rise Ochsner hangs in the place of honor at the Upperline.

His long career included numerous other restaurants in New York City, Long Island, and finally, happily, in New Orleans.

(recipe continued from left)
carefully to the Dutch oven and fry them, in batches, until golden brown. Divide the oysters among the baked bread rounds, drizzle with another 1/4 cup of the Maitre d'Hôtel Butter, and garnish with lemon and parsley. Serve immediately.

Owner, JoAnn Clevenger has made the Upperline her home, and she is the welcoming hostess. She is fond of saying that "New Orleans is extraordinarily beautiful. Look at the music we have, the architecture, the flowers.

We're very lucky. And you know, it's not just where you're going, but the in between part—how you get here—that matters." Dining at the Upperline is one of the ways to get there.

CHEF DAVE BRIDGES, UPPERLINE RESTAURANT
CLASSIC GARLIC *and* BREAD SOUP

The Upperline's annual garlic festival makes certain that no creatures of the night wander around the kicky uptown establishment. It is important to completely cook the garlic to release the sweet mellow flavor.

SERVES 8

2 tablespoons butter
2 tablespoons olive oil
6 cups sliced yellow onions
2 cups garlic cloves
1 tablespoon fresh thyme leaves
2 tablespoons fresh tarragon leaves
7 cups chicken stock
2 bay leaves
3 cups cubed stale French bread with crust removed
1 cup heavy cream
salt and white pepper to taste
fried oysters and thin brie slices for garnish, if desired

1. In a medium-sized heavy-bottomed pot, heat the butter and oil over medium heat. Add the onion and garlic and cook, stirring frequently, until they are golden brown. Add the thyme, tarragon, 6 cups of the chicken stock, and bay leaves and bring to a boil. Stir in the bread cubes and simmer for 10 minutes, or until the bread has softened. Remove from heat, let cool for 10 minutes, and discard the bay leaves.

2. Pour the soup into a blender or food processor and process until completely smooth. Return the soup to the pot and heat through. If the mixture is too thick, stir in enough of the remaining chicken stock to reach the desired consistency. Whisk in the cream and season with the salt and white pepper.

For an optional garnish, place a fried oyster or two on top of the soup in individual oven-safe bowls. Lay a thin slice of brie over the oysters and broil under a preheated broiler until the cheese has just melted.

CHEF JOHN FOLSE, RESTAURANT R'EVOLUTION, ROYAL SONESTA

DEATH BY GUMBO

Boneless quail is used for this recipe, however bone-in birds are fine (though result in a little more work when eating) if boneless is not available. Chef John Folse created this most special gumbo for Craig Claiborne of The New York Times. It's a decadent, sublime take on regional sensibilities.

Elegance brushes elbows with grace, and Louisiana's different cultural groups mix without losing their individual flavors. Demonstrating powerful tastes with restraint, Folse melds culinary styles for an elegant menu. We may think of gumbo as a casual, however welcome, meal but he elevates the comforting mélange with a whole quail nesting over the bowlful of tradition.

Folse and fellow chef, Rick Tramonto, founder of acclaimed fine dining restaurants in Chicago, together opened Restaurant R'evolution. The French Quarter establishment is Folse's entry into New Orleans as a contemporary Creole extravaganza. They call it modern, imaginative reinterpretation of classic Cajun and Creole cuisine. We call it dinner.

SERVES 6

FOR THE QUAIL

6 boneless Bobwhite quail
salt and freshly ground pepper to taste
3/4 cup cooked white rice
1/2 teaspoon filé powder
1 tablespoon chopped parsley
six 1/8-inch-thick slices of
   andouille sausage
6 oysters, poached in their own liquid

FOR THE GUMBO

1/2 cup vegetable oil
3/4 cup flour
1 cup diced onion
1 cup diced celery
1/2 cup diced red bell pepper
1/8 cup minced garlic
1/2 cup sliced mushrooms
1/4 cup sliced tasso ham
1 1/2 quarts chicken stock
1/2 teaspoon dried thyme
salt and freshly ground pepper to taste
1/2 cup sliced scallions
1/2 cup chopped parsley

Prepare the Quail

1. Season each bird inside and out with salt and pepper.

2. In a small mixing bowl, season the rice with salt, pepper, filé powder, and parsley.

3. Stuff the cavity of each quail with 1 tablespoon of seasoned rice, 1 slice of andouille, 1 oyster, and another tablespoon of seasoned rice. Cover the birds

(recipe continued at right)

(recipe continued from left)

with plastic wrap and set aside.

Make the Gumbo

1. In a 2-gallon stockpot set over medium-high heat, warm the oil. Add the flour and cook, stirring constantly to make sure that the mixture does not burn, until a dark brown roux forms.

2. Add the onion, celery, bell pepper, and garlic and sauté them in the roux for about 3 to 5 minutes, or until they are wilted.

3. Add the mushrooms and ham and cook for another 3 minutes.

4. Add the chicken stock, one ladle at a time to allow the mixture to heat back up between ladlefuls. When all the stock has been incorporated, stir in the thyme and salt and pepper to taste.

5. Place the prepared stuffed quail in the gumbo and simmer, covered, for 30 minutes. The quail are finished when they are tender and the legs separate from the body easily. Transfer them to a platter and keep warm.

6. Strain the gumbo through a fine sieve into another saucepan to remove all seasonings. Add the quail, scallions, and parsley to the pan and return to a low boil until heated through.

7. To serve, spoon one quail into each of 6 bowls and ladle the rest of the gumbo around it.

(recipe continued from right)

Add to the ramekins, filling to about I inch above the top of the rims. With a spoon, smooth and shape the tops into domes so that the edges of the domes are touching the rims of the ramekins.

5. Bake immediately for 20 minutes, or until the top has turned golden brown.

Prepare the whiskey sauce while the soufflés are baking.

Make the Whiskey Sauce

1. In a small saucepan over medium heat, bring the cream to a boil. In a small mixing bowl, mix the cornstarch and water together. Add the cornstarch mixture to the pan and bring back to a boil, whisking to mix thoroughly. Remove from heat.

2. While the cream mixture is still warm, whisk in the sugar and bourbon until they are fully incorporated. Let cool to room temperature.

3. When the soufflés are finished, place each ramekin on a small plate or saucer. Poke a small hole in the top of each soufflé and fill with whiskey sauce. Serve immediately.

CHEF TORY MCPHAIL, COMMANDER'S PALACE
BREAD PUDDING SOUFFLÉ

Celebrate a grand finale with a culinary sleight of hand, delicious magic. It doesn't fall.

SERVES 6

FOR THE BREAD PUDDING
3/4 cup granulated sugar
1 teaspoon ground cinnamon
pinch of nutmeg
3 large eggs
1 cup heavy cream
1 teaspoon vanilla extract
5 cups 1-inch cubes of crumb of
  French bread
butter to grease baking pan and ramekins
1/3 cup raisins (optional)

FOR THE MERINGUE
9 large egg whites, room temperature
1/4 teaspoon cream of tartar
3/4 cup granulated sugar

FOR THE WHISKEY SAUCE
1 cup heavy whipping cream
1/2 tablespoon cornstarch
1 tablespoon water, room temperature
3 tablespoons granulated sugar
1/4 cup bourbon

Make the Bread Pudding

1. Preheat the oven to 350 degrees.

2. In a large mixing bowl, combine the sugar, cinnamon, and nutmeg. Slowly add the eggs, one at a time, whisking thoroughly, and whisk in the cream and vanilla. Add the bread cubes, tossing to coat evenly. Let stand for 10 minutes to allow the bread to absorb the liquid.

3. Use the butter to grease the bottom of a 8-inch-square baking pan and 6 ramekins. Place the raisins in the bottom of the pan (if you're using them) and cover them with the egg and bread mixture.

4. Bake for 25 to 30 minutes, or until the top is golden brown. A toothpick inserted in the center should come out clean. Let cool to room temperature.

Make the Meringue and Soufflé

1. In a large, clean mixing bowl, beat the egg whites with the cream of tartar until foamy.

2. Gradually add the sugar while continuing to beat the eggs. Continue beating until shiny and peaks form.

3. Cut the cooled bread pudding in half. Break one half into pieces in a medium mixing bowl. Add 1/4 of the meringue to the bowl and fold together gently. Divide equally among the 6 greased ramekins.

4. Break the remaining half of the bread pudding into pieces and fold into the remaining meringue.

(recipe continued at left)

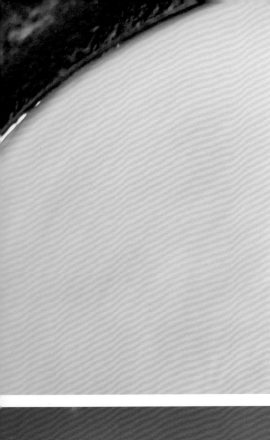

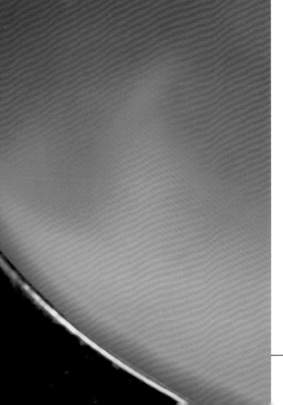

ROUX

Roux is the magical thickener and flavoring necessary for many gumbos, stews, and soups in Louisiana cooking. Making roux is not nearly as difficult as it may sound and can approach a Zen-like experience for a dedicated cook. Depending on skill and speed, creating a light ("blond") roux can take a few minutes and a dark roux up to 45 minutes to an hour.

The great news is that roux freezes beautifully. So make a large batch, cool it, then apportion it into small containers and freeze it for future use.

A roux is nothing more than flour browned in oil or fat, and it delivers much more flavor than that would suggest. The raw flour taste is eliminated in the final product, and the chemical reaction created by the flour browning in the hot oil imparts a nutty, smoky flavor that deepens as the roux becomes darker. The scent as the reaction begins is distinctive and appetizing.

A Creole or Cajun roux begins with flour and oil or fat in equal proportions. Some cooks prefer a thicker roux, using more flour than oil. The language of roux pertains to its different hues, which can range from a barely colored tan to the color of peanut butter and through café au lait to dark mahogany. Before choosing the oil or fat, decide on the flavor and color of roux you're seeking. For example, a blond roux's flavor is more subtle but has higher thickening power than a dark roux.

temperatures, so unless it is clarified and the solids skimmed off, it will not work easily for a darker roux.

While white all-purpose flour is the norm, whole-wheat flour imparts a splendid nutty taste. The 1-to-1 ratio of oil and flour is standard, although some cooks prefer a bit more flour than oil, as much as 1/2 a cup on a one cup to one cup measurement.

Begin the process by turning on some music (for entertainment while you're stirring) and assembling the necessary equipment. The ideal basic tools are a comfortable wire whisk and a cast-iron skillet or Dutch oven. Thin metal pots significantly increase the risk of scorching.

Start the roux by heating the oil on medium-low heat. Add the flour slowly, stirring the mixture continuously with a whisk or a wooden spoon. Be patient and take your time. Once the oil and flour begin to emulsify and bubble, the heat level can be raised or lowered. But this calls for diligence. The color stays deceptively the same for some minutes, then changes rapidly. The flour can scorch before you're able to react. (There is no saving a scorched roux. It is over, it is finished, and it must be trashed.)

Once the roux starts to approach the desired color level, remove it from the flame a shade or two lighter than you want and continue whisking, since the flour will continue to cook quickly and darken further.

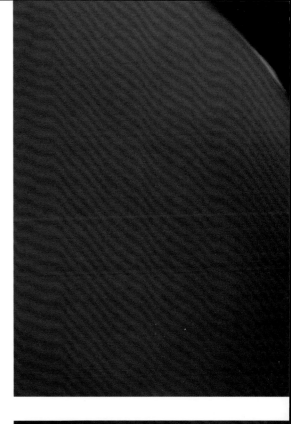

SEASONINGS

CREOLE SEASONING
MAKES 1 cup

3 tablespoons paprika
2 tablespoons onion powder
2 tablespoons garlic powder
2 tablespoons dried oregano
2 tablespoons dried basil
1 tablespoon dried thyme

1 tablespoon black peppercorns, freshly ground
1 tablespoon white peppercorns, freshly ground
1 tablespoon cayenne pepper
1 tablespoon kosher salt, optional
dash of chili powder
dash of cumin powder

Mix all ingredients well in a small bowl. Store in an airtight container until ready to use.

BLACKENED SEASONING BLEND
MAKES 1 cup

3 tablespoons paprika
2 tablespoons onion powder
2 tablespoons garlic powder
2 tablespoons dried oregano
2 tablespoons dried basil
1 tablespoon dried thyme

1 tablespoon black peppercorns, freshly ground
1 tablespoon white peppercorns, freshly ground
1 tablespoon cayenne pepper
1 tablespoon kosher salt, optional
dash of chili powder
dash of cumin powder

Mix all ingredients well in a small bowl. Store in an airtight container until ready to use.

POULTRY SEASONING
MAKES 1/4 cup

3 teaspoons kosher or sea salt
1 teaspoon paprika
1/2 teaspoon onion powder
1/2 teaspoon garlic powder
freshly ground black peppercorns
freshly ground white peppercorns

1/2 teaspoon cayenne pepper
1/2 teaspoon dried rosemary
1/2 teaspoon dried sage leaves
1/2 teaspoon dried oregano
1/2 teaspoon dried thyme

Mix all ingredients well in a small bowl. Store in an airtight container until ready to use.

ROUX *and the* TRINITY

If you intend to use the roux for gumbo, you'll want to add the "Trinity" of Creole-Cajun cooking—chopped onion, celery and bell pepper. While the addition of these vegetables will cause the roux to darken, it also begins cooling the roux as the vegetables cook and release their liquids. Once the vegetables have softened, gradually begin stirring in the stock or other liquid. Of course, some chefs reverse the process, cooking the vegetables in the oil then adding the roux. Chef Donald Link's recipe for shrimp and grits uses this method.

The proportions among the Trinity's components can vary according to the cook's fancy, as well as the cook's personal preferences among them and what happens to be in the refrigerator at a given moment. Essentially, however, the Trinity is:

2 parts onion, chopped
1 part celery, chopped
1/3 part green* bell pepper, chopped

Many recipes call for bell peppers in their confetti colors of green, yellow, red and orange. There are no flavor or textural differences among them, so use whichever you prefer.

Once the vegetables are chopped, combined and set aside, prepare the roux. When the roux has been cooked to a shade or two under what you're seeking, carefully begin stirring in the Trinity. When the vegetables hit the hot roux they will splatter, so add them slowly and stand back from the skillet. When the vegetables have been completely incorporated into the roux, the flour will darken even more. Allow the mixture to simmer until the vegetables release their liquids and the onions are translucent.

At this point, slowly add the stock or water, stirring as it is blended. Louisiana cookbook author Marcelle Bienvenu, whose vast experience makes her an expert in these matters, prefers to heat the liquid before adding it. This works well.

From the very beginning of the cooking process, the quality of the roux, Trinity and stock is most important for a gumbo's full-bodied flavor. A word of caution about seafood gumbo: Reserve the delicately flavored raw oysters, shrimp, fish or crawfish until the gumbo is just a few minutes from being removed from heat. Otherwise, the seafood will overcook and become tough and tasteless. The same applies to other proteins such as

sausage, chicken and duck. Give them enough time to cook at the end, but don't leech out their flavor by overcooking.

INDEX

ACKNOWLEDGEMENTS

Our chefs and their staffs make it possible and make it happen. Eat here, and eat often. Then talk about our restaurants, plan your next meal, and make more reservations.

Fiercely talented photographers contributed many images, including Paul Rico's crawfish, groceries, and gumbo; Mary Lou Uttermohlen's cityscapes, people, and Mardi Gras images; Sam Hanna's King Cake for Sucré New Orleans; Barry Garner's French Quarter Festival; and Sally Ekman's Jazz Fest. They have my gratitude. Art director Michael Lauve continues to be a rock, maintaining a calm serenity.

Senior editor Elaine Richard edited recipes and made them make sense, as an editor should. Maura Kaye-Casella is a spectacular literary agent, and Chris Rose writes a wicked forward. Just about everything he writes is wicked.

Barry Garner is our ace production chief and also did three or four different technical jobs, as a photographer and camera assistant, cook, organizer, and mind-reader—hard duty from start to finish. Chef Brandon Canizaro cooked his best along with Chef Raquel Oliveira. Chef Tommy DiGiovanni freely gave advice. My testing and tasting Facebook friends did delicious work, what fun. Authors Grace Bauer, and Erin Hicks were always here with smiles and moral support. Eloisa Zepeda kept us all in order, with her brand-new daughter, tiny, sweet Amberly.

Once again, the terrific people at Pelican Publishing were delightful to work with, especially Johanna Rotondo-McCord and Abi Pollokoff. As always, Pelican's production and sales staff were stellar. Everyone weighed in with support. Each and every person has my appreciation.

My beloved family always seems to get neglected as much as I adore them, but then they forgive me. Thanks to my sisters and my brothers. While I wasn't looking, their children graduated with varying degrees in biomedical engineering, psychology, nursing, and anthropology. How proud can an aunt be?

Our booksellers are the lifeblood of the business, and enough thanks never seem to go their way. So, thank you, thank you again.

Finally, my love goes to Billy, my husband.